"VACANCY —You Are Urgently Needed" is an excellent read regardless of your level of experience or position. Whether you're a student or teacher, start-up entrepreneur or conglomerate CEO, civil servant or political leader, it provides simple and practical advice not just for the job search process but also for life, business and society.

This book provides the tools for solving problems that have worried individuals and organizations for decades —how to fulfil the fullness of purpose —be it getting the right job, building the right business, raising the right family or transforming a nation. It provides an innovative and interesting way for the reader to self-assess and develop the proper life perspective and competencies to be successful in any sphere of life. Recommended reading.

- Oluwatosin Thomas Okojie

(CEO, Total Ascent)

"VACANCY —You Are Urgently Needed" is a simply set out reference book with easy to understand principles that will help clarify the needs of an employer to millions of not only job seekers but those already in employment who may be desirous of an elevation in their career.

It is definitely a must read for prospective employees as early as the teenage years as the truths expounded are truths that some in the labour force have not yet grasped even after many years of working

1

life. This book definitely has the potential of cutting down years of fruitless labour at the altar of employment for those fortunate to imbibe its principles.

Even for someone who has been in employment for the best part of 15 years, I had quite a few "Aha!" light bulb moments while reading it.

- Amina Sijuwade, Organization and Management Consultant (Presently Commissioner of Justice and Attorney General Kaduna State)

Finally, a painful yet truthful picture of how to start or excel in a career has been recorded in the simplest narrative, devoid of many clichés of today's so called motivational literature. The book inspires a new personal paradigm and a deep sense of renewal especially for all those who genuinely aspire to take that next step into achievement in life. Anedge and Folorunso have produced an invaluable manual that will certainly engage every willing mind to make that change for the better.

- Adebambo Adewopo, Professor of Intellectual Property Law (Former DG Copyright Commission)

I've got to admit: this is a compendium of useful nuggets…The structure of the chapters are consistent: with leading quotes, main texts, summary highlights and suggested actions that answer the question "what pragmatic thing should I take away and do?" …In conclusion, this is a brilliant piece of work.

- Shittu Olatunji Shittu, Chartered I T Professional (British Petroleum UK)

VACANCY

You Are Urgently Needed

BECOME HIGH IN DEMAND. EARN MORE AND ENRICH YOUR LIFE.

ANEDGE EKIOTENNE & FOLORUNSO ALIU

3

A catalogue copy of this book is available at the

National Library of Nigeria

ISBN: 978-1540462091

PUBLISHERS CONTACT

Plot B41 Pentville 1 Estate, Lokogoma, FCT, Abuja.

+ 234 818 929 2842, +234 809 189 2922

Email: anedgelive@gmail.com

aliu@thevacancyproject.com

DEDICATION

To my wife, my best friend, number one fan, best critic

and motivator, *Abigail Ekiotenne.*

You are amazing.

And to my genius son, *Carmiel B. Ekiotenne.*

And my darling daughter Adriel T. Ekiotenne

You both make me feel so blessed.

To my wife, my best friend, greatest critic and jewel of inestimable
value, *Olujoke Aliu,*

My daughter and princess, *Ireifeoluwa Aliu,*

My son, my strength, *Eriifeoluwa Aliu,*

And to the big man of the house, my son, *Eniifeoluwa Aliu.*

You all make it worthwhile.

ACKNOWLEDGEMENTS

Writing this book on employees, employability, value creation and entrepreneurship has indeed been a long journey. We are grateful that the product of the journey is finally here. The reality of several years of work experience, coupled with research, writing, consulting and thinking is the book you now hold in your hands.

We are grateful to everyone who has been involved in the process of writing and publishing this book. We wish to specifically thank the following people for their immense and unforgettable contribution:

We thank our wives who let us spend several hours at the writing desks and for being our greatest critics. Our children have also been of great joy to us in the writing of this book.

Our profound gratitude goes to Chief (Honourable) Chukwuemeka Chikelu (former Minister of Information) for his thorough and candid feedback on the first draft of this book —Dear Sir, the book now reads more Nigerian. Mr. Kudla Milinda Satumari, an entrepreneur and business mogul, your support, practical insight and business perspective shows through in the successes of your business and we hope the readers get to have such successes after reading this book. Professor Adebambo Adewopo (the pioneer Nigerian Professor of Intellectual Property Law and former Director General Nigerian Copyrights Commission), your encouragement and insight have been a major boost for us. Our dear Pastor Israel W. Abam (Senior Pastor, Guiding Light Assembly, Abuja Worship Center), we thank you for not only providing spiritual guidance but also for being actively involved in the successful completion of this work. Honourable Commissioner of

Justice and Attorney General (Kaduna State), Mrs. Amina Sijuwade, you painstakingly went through every chapter of this book and presented comments and suggestions on every page. Your detailed and in-depth analyses were simply priceless. Mrs. Grace Omo-Lamai (Director of Human Resources, Nigerian Bottling Company), you provided us awesome insight into the mind and perspective of the employer. Your suggestions went a long way into making this book better. Mrs. Adepele Williams (PhD), you provided us an international perspective and what goes into making a book of this nature internationally relevant. For this we are most grateful. Mr. Thomas Okojie (Chief Executive Officer, Total Ascent), your understanding of local and international human capital development needs went a long way to making this book complete. Mr. Shittu Olatunji Shittu (Chartered IT Professional, BP, UK), your research angle was priceless. Mr Ifeanyi Ukoha (Interswitch Ltd. Northern Regional Executive), we appreciate your enthusiastic encouragement all through the process of writing this book, and to Miss Doris Adaugo Uche, your fresh perspective certainly added life to the final product. Mrs Olayinka Adefope, our teacher and friend, we thank you for helping us to clarify the focus of this book. We also wish to thank our editor, Uche Okonkwo, your professional touch made all the difference. We thank and acknowledge all friends and families that have contributed to the successful completion of this book.

Finally, we thank God for His inspiration and all He has endowed us with to be able to complete this book. Indeed, we are eternally grateful.

Contents

INTRODUCTION

THE PATH TO YOUR REWARD

Why are some people highly sought after by employers/customers, while others struggle to get jobs or sell their goods and services? Why do some people get promoted while their colleagues stagnate or even get fired? Why are some people paid large sums of money while others barely survive on what they earn? Why do some get the rewards they desire while others get little or nothing? What are the differentiating factors?

Those who end up getting the rewards they desire start by asking, 'What problem can I solve?' 'What much-needed value can I create or provide for employers/customers?' Any person that is highly sought after operates with this mindset. All true achievements attained, and rewards earned, are as a result of being able to solve a problem. Your success and happiness in life depends on your willingness to help someone solve their problems. Successful people in every field think of the solutions they can offer. This is the path to achieving whatever reward you desire.

Problems abound all over the world. Some problems are universal while others vary according to circumstances. Problems are diverse and often complex. They range from issues such as global warming, unemployment, terrorism, epidemics and environmental pollution to the need for faster and better means of transportation. They include the need for faster and better means of communication, the need for effective business management processes, domestic needs such as cooking a meal, doing laundry, washing a car, cleaning a house etc. They could be organizational or personal in nature.

All human interaction is aimed toward solving a problem or

meeting a need. People wake up every day to deal with old and new problems. Everyone wakes up to either look for solutions to their problems or be the solution to other people's problems. Businesses are established to make profit through the provision of solutions in the form of goods or services. Leaders influence people and provide direction to solving the problems in their organization or nation. However, in this age of fast food and quick fixes, people want to make gains without solving problems. People talk of get-rich-quick schemes that provide no meaningful solutions. Some people provide little or no value to society but expect to be paid lots of money. People offer sub-standard services and products that do not solve employers'/customers' problems and expect a demand for their products and services. Some employees want to be paid more without providing value-added services that solve the problems of their employer.

University graduates want to be employed and paid large sums of money without investing time in developing relevant knowledge and skills that will position them as solution providers. Note that the purpose of education is to teach the human mind to learn to solve problems. The Greek etymology of the word 'education' is derived from two root words, 'E' and 'duco'. The term 'E' means 'out of' and 'duco' means 'to lead'. Every man has inherent and latent potential. Education is primarily designed to teach the human mind the ability to bring forth (lead out) from within solutions to problems. The startling truth is that there is only one job position available anywhere —that of the problem solver. The title attached to the position does not really matter; it merely describes the problem(s) the bearer must solve. There are lots of problems around us, and where there are problems there are definitely opportunities to create valuable solutions and earn rewards.

Your success depends on your ability to discover and solve problems.

In this book, we use the words 'employer/customer' to refer to the group or individual with problems that require solutions. The employer/customer can be an individual, a company, a community or a country. You are employed by whomsoever you provide service to. The president of a country is employed through election by the citizens of his country. The president solves the problem of direction through visionary leadership that should create wealth and prosperity for the country. The CEO of a company is employed by the board to solve the problem of providing strategic direction and management to make the company prosperous. Businessmen and women are employed by their customers to solve various types of problems. A company's staff members are employed by the company to solve its problems, and the problems of its customers.

If you develop the right mindset, work to acquire the tools as detailed in this book, and apply them appropriately and consistently, you are setting yourself up to achieve great things. If you will provide the required solutions for employers or customers there is a vacancy for you, regardless of your current situation. This applies to new graduates seeking employment, experienced workers seeking new opportunities for growth, and prospective entrepreneurs.

We have taken a critical look at our environment and have seen the need to bring to the fore the fundamental principles that will help you position yourself as a highly sought after solution provider. We have compiled these principles in this book as a single reference source, placing adequate emphasis on key concepts that will help anyone who is willing to put them to use.

This book in your hand is the beginning of a journey. It is a presentation of some of the best ideas that, if applied, will help you clarify your path and align your thoughts and actions towards being the one who is sought after. The clock is ticking. You cannot afford to hesitate.

Chapter One

SORRY, NO VACANCY

A farmer who will not work in the rain or under the sun will have nothing to harvest at the end of the farming season.

- Nigerian proverb

Sorry, no vacancy! When you are not given the job after the interview, it means *sorry, no vacancy*. When you do not get the promotion or raise, it means *sorry, no vacancy*. If you ever hear the words 'You are fired', it means *sorry, no vacancy*. When a customer refuses to contract you for your service, it means *sorry no vacancy*. Many times when you are told there is no vacancy, or when you see a sign that reads 'no vacancy', it could mean that there is a vacancy but just not for you (at least not at that time). Have you ever considered that YOU might be responsible for this 'no vacancy'? Understandably, you would deny this. You may get defensive and point the blame at other people. This reaction is an infection we have termed 'blamisitis'. We define blamisitis as the inflammation of the 'blame centre' which leads to the denial of responsibility for your situations, predicaments and misfortunes. Blamisitis is what makes people blame everyone and every circumstance for their predicament except themselves. Most people would rather blame the government, the economy, the educational system, lack of connections, corruption, the environment, lack of infrastructure, the clergy, employers, customers, their parents and, for some, even their ancestors. People often blame everyone and everything they can think of, except themselves.

You probably have reasons why you think you are not to blame. However, you may in fact be responsible for the 'no vacancy,' 'you are fired' or 'no deal' responses you get. There are hundreds and thousands of people who have encountered similar or worse situations and limitations than yours. Some of these people are now being told daily, 'You are urgently needed'. Think about this: even while companies downsize, retrench and right-size they keep certain people and also hire others. Why? What makes the difference? The desired groups of people take personal responsibility. They refuse to allow the prevailing circumstance act on them. They choose to act rather than be acted upon.

At the extreme of this spectrum are cases where life seems to hand down a 'no vacancy' verdict from birth. You might get sympathy, empathy and understanding from people; however, we dare say that even when it appears that life itself is against you, you are still ultimately responsible for your final outcome.

THE FINAL OUTCOME IS YOURS TO DETERMINE

There he was living on the dumpsite along with many other scavengers. They slept, ate, bathed, lived together; a whole community of scavengers. They had come from all over the nation: orphans, children with no one to provide care, and adults looking to eke out a living by collecting and selling recyclable materials. These scavengers lived in Lagos, existing alongside the opulence of the 'Centre of Excellence' but unable to touch it. Most of them only thought about getting their next meal and a place to lay their heads after the day's work, under the ramshackle makeshift structures they built on the dumpsite. No one blamed them for their predicament. Life had dealt them a bad hand. Society understood their plight and neither demanded nor expected anything of them. They were not expected to rise above their estate in life. It was okay to be poor —in fact, it was expected of them.

He was dealt the same blow by fate as most of the other

15

scavengers; maybe even worse. He grew up in the harsh, crime-infested environment of Ajegunle. He had to drop out of secondary school due to financial constraints; he was left to fend for himself on the streets, and he ended up at the dumpsite. He was different from the others in one aspect, however; he was determined to look beyond his misery. Of course he had to sleep on the dumpsite and he went to work gathering recyclable materials like all the others, but he was known to be passionate about something else —music. As a scavenger, he sold his salvaged materials and could barely feed himself but he saved his earnings to pay for studio time to produce a music album. He would rather be known as a musician than as a scavenger. He wore a constant smile and took special care to look clean and presentable for his studio time.

One day, a BBC documentary producer happened on this young man at the dumpsite. He was handed a camera to film his daily struggles as a scavenger. He did a good job of showing the life of a scavenger, but he did not stop there. He showcased his talent as a musician and spoke about his dream and all he was doing to become a recording artiste. He showed his struggles and aspirations, leveraging on the opportunity that had come his way —and voila, everything changed. His story was featured on Part 1 of the BBC documentary, *Welcome to Lagos*, aired on BBC 2.

He has since become popular and has released songs on iTunes. He has been featured in *The Punch* newspaper in Nigeria, *The Observer*, *The Independent* and *The London Metro* in the UK. He has also featured on *Heart of the Matter*, a TV program anchored by Pastor Wale Adefarasin of Guiding Light Assembly. He has travelled to the UK, where on September 4, 2010 he performed in front of over 30,000 guests at the O2 Arena, and returned to Nigeria to set up various projects to help children of indigent background and raise them out of poverty by providing education.

His name: Eric Obuh, also known as Vocal Slender. Life dealt him a bad hand, but he made the best of it.

Only one person can transform your life, determine your happiness, outlook to life and path to success. That person is you. You are the only person that can create the environment for your inner self to succeed. Others may help, but you are the primary driver on the road to success and happiness. You are the number one change agent for your life. Your life changes when you change. It changes when you realize that you are the only one responsible for your life. Until you realize this, sorry, no vacancy!

James Allen in his book, *As a Man Thinketh*, sums it up:

Man is buffeted by circumstance so long as he believes himself to be the creature of outside conditions, but when he realizes that he is a creative power, and that he may command the hidden soil and seeds of his being out of which circumstances grow, he then becomes the rightful master of himself.

Sometimes you will not get what you desire or deserve, even when you put in your best efforts. Sometimes, you may even be denied what is clearly yours. You worked hard, you gave it your best, you were even commended as the very best for the job or opening, but somehow and due to unknown circumstances you were denied the opportunity. This is possible, but it does not happen very often for those who have prepared and have taken responsibility. The issue is not that this

17

happened to you. The issue is, would you choose to allow this determine how far you go, or your sense of self-worth? You may not be in control of the situation but you are responsible for how you respond to it.

The truth is that once you are prepared and you take responsibility, you will most likely be better than any job or position you take or leave. In other words, your worth is not tied to whether you were cheated out of a job or not. What matters is your attitude right after it happens. This needs to be re-emphasized: people who are prepared and who take responsibility are not often cheated out of their opportunities. When you know this you will be better prepared to rebound and better positioned to prove your mettle whenever you get the opportunity.

It is true that you cannot change the circumstances, the seasons or the wind, but you can change yourself. That is something within your control. Failing to accept responsibility and attempting to shift the blame for the results in your life onto other people, institutions and situations will only undermine your character and weaken your resolve.

I once saw a poster that read: "If life shows you pepper, make pepper soup." This is an insightful statement. Instead of letting the pepper discomfort you, make the most of it. You have to take responsibility for creating your opportunities. If opportunity comes knocking, open the door and answer it. If it doesn't come knocking, go looking for it. If you can't find it, build a door of opportunity, knock on it and answer it. Whatever happens, you are responsible for making it happen.

YOU WORK FOR YOURSELF

You always have the choice to do what you want to do, and you can decide how much money you want to make doing it. The idea of a job is to provide a product or service for which you will be rewarded. In the employer-employee arrangement, you sell your services temporarily to an employer in return for a pay check (reward), but ultimately you have the power to decide who you sell your services to, and for how long. Because you have this choice, it means you work for no other person but yourself. You are self-employed.

You choose your employer, not the other way around. You applied to do a job for your employer. You chose to gain the skills necessary to attract an employer to pay for your services; therefore, you are the CEO of an enterprise —The Enterprise of Me. You have one employee —YOU. Every other person is your customer. Your employer is your customer. You are responsible for selling one product —YOU. If your product is not selling you are solely responsible.

In selling your services, you must decide the reasons you are selling yourself (your skill, knowledge, personality, network, ability etc.) to a particular employer/customer, and if it is the right solution they need. Why should an employer/customer buy your service? Are your skills relevant to solving their problems? How? As the CEO of YOU Incorporated, you are totally responsible for the success or failure of your product —YOU.

YOU ARE AN ENTREPRENEUR

As the head of your corporation, your business is to make a profit by solving problems for employers/customers. Your commitment is to establish yourself as a leader in delivering solutions of high value. To deliver appropriate solutions, you need to know the needs of employers/customers and get the requisite skills required to meet those needs. If you can prove that you can solve a besetting problem for an organization, customer or your community, you will get hired and rewarded accordingly.

CEOs of ME enterprises are intensely result-oriented. They take high levels of initiative. They volunteer for assignments and they are always asking for more responsibilities. As a result, they become highly valuable people to organizations, customers, communities and countries. They continually prepare themselves for the future and for positions of higher authority by the solution provider mindset they have developed. Problem solving is one of the most highly valued qualities you can have as the CEO of ME enterprise. No matter the era you always get a vacancy.

To illustrate this, here is a story of a Nigerian who worked with the 'CEO of ME' mindset. As a fourth year Information and Communication Technology (ICT) student in the University, it was mandatory for Oloruntola to proceed on a six-month industrial training program with an ICT company, as stipulated by the Industrial Training Fund policy for engineering students.

The first placement he got was quite comfortable as he was well respected and considered quite an asset. His monthly stipend was N10, 000, which was quite a tidy sum at the time. He was, however, not satisfied after two months because he was the only technical person in the department, which meant he essentially had to teach himself for six months.

Oloruntola wanted to learn and focus on imbibing value. He therefore decided to apply to one of the leading companies providing cutting edge ICT solutions in Nigeria. When he was asked to start, the stipend paid by the company was N1,500 compared to the N10,000 which he was used to. On his resumption, the stipend was increased to N2,500 for the seventeen (17) ICT industrial training students with the company at the time.

The company had a standing structure and hierarchy —the GM in charge of all technical solutions and deployment had a team of seasoned ICT engineers who were in charge of specific projects. These engineers in turn had technical experts who reported to them. After this group came the freshly graduated engineers and National Youth Service Corp (NYSC) engineers. At the bottom of the totem pole was the pool of Industrial Training students who were to learn from the hierarchy. Project meetings were held every weekend. At these meetings, the progress of each project was presented by the chief engineer. Questions were posed to the different members of the team on the project to ensure everyone understood the project and the technical details. Most importantly, it was a time to ensure the projects were on track for delivery in terms of quality and time. It was not the place of an industrial trainee to lead a team or manage a project.

After two months of working with one of the best engineers in the company on a complex project and taking initiatives in ensuring delivery, Oloruntola consistently took on tasks and responsibilities as he got better understanding and grasp of the technical and project management requirements on the project he was assigned. His direct supervisor gradually began to allow him take on more responsibilities in the delivery of the project while he focused on other issues within the office. After a while, Oloruntola became the face of the ICT firm to the customer and he managed the requests and expectations while providing adequate feedback and technical details to both sides (his company and the customer). The project was successfully delivered and documentation provided to the customer. He went as far as ensuring that the customer was enthusiastic about paying for the job done.

Just a month before the end of his ICT industrial training, during one of the weekend project meetings, Oloruntola requested that he be allowed to manage a project on his own. This created shockwaves in the meeting, especially amongst the ICT trainee pool who were amazed that Oloruntola was biting off more than he could chew. This had never happened before and it went against the established norm. However, the GM had noticed the young ICT trainee, and so had a few seasoned engineers who agreed with the GM that Oloruntola could be given a project to execute on his own. It should, however, be a project that was not too strategic, such that if it did fail it would not set the company back financially.

Before Oloruntola returned to school, he had almost completed the project, with recommendations from the customer. A newly recruited Youth Corps engineer was attached to his project. The Corps member was to learn from him and ultimately take over the project as he prepared to go back to campus. When Oloruntola finished his industrial training the GM assured him of a position in the company if he did return after his studies.

After graduation, his National Youth Service Corps posting was to a school in another state to teach Mathematics. When he realized that he could not get through to the students (most of them could not speak English) and he knew he was not adding value to himself or the students, he redeployed to Lagos and went back to the company where he had done his Industrial Training. As at this time, there was no vacancy. The entire slot for NYSC had been filled. The GM had to provide special justification for the engagement of Oloruntola. He had to stick his neck out for him to be brought on board.

As a Youth Corps member he was entrusted with

responsibilities meant for very seasoned professionals because he always requested such assignments. He quickly became a core member of the delivery team. At a certain time, many of the senior engineers in the company got opportunities and relocated abroad. Thereafter, the delivery of most of the very technical projects fell on Oloruntola and a few of the personnel. This became a turning point as he was assigned a lot of very important projects while he was also required to get the necessary professional certification required to deliver on those projects.

Oloruntola was not only interested in the management of technical solutions but also people and financial management. When his supervisor noticed this, he was challenged to take up roles and responsibilities within two years of being with the company as a middle-level manager. Within three years, he had been moved into different departments to take charge of different technical and people management roles.

At the end of three years, he was already at the same level of roles and position as personnel who had been in the company for over seven years before he joined the company. After seven years, he was appointed managing director of the company. A guiding principle he holds is that, "one should take responsibility. Every opportunity should be used to add value to yourself knowing that you work for yourself."

ENGAGE IN THE PROBLEM SOLVING EQUATION

Every successful individual engages in the problem solving equation. Adeola Adeboye (Wiseman Apparel), Richard Branson (Virgin), Aliko Dangote (Dangote Group), Mike Adenuga (Glo), Mark Zuckerberg (Facebook), Larry Page and Sergey Brin (Google), Bill Gates (Microsoft), Dr. Cosmas Maduka (Coscharis Group) Donald Trump

(The Trump Organization), Steve Jobs (Apple), Ben Murray-Bruce (Silverbird) and many others are taking care of challenges that people want to desperately get rid of or providing the much needed solutions that improve people's lives or businesses —that's how they get their rewards.

Businesses are built by solving problems, and so the search is always on for people who will help solve problems better and faster, thereby increasing profits. Employers/customers have problems, and so they are willing to pay whoever they perceive as the one with the solution. If you work for an organization and you stop solving valuable problems for your employer, it's just a matter of time before you get fired. You get fired because you have become dead weight (a problem).

In a market full of underperforming employees, employers and customers are desperately looking for the right fit — people who will address their challenges. That's why problem solving ability regularly ranks as one of the most desirable traits in a prospective employee. Solution providers are strategic and critical thinkers; people who bring ideas and solutions. And guess what? Ideas and solutions *make money*. So if you choose not to be personally responsible for providing solutions for people, *sorry, no vacancy*. Your best option is to take responsibility and become a problem solver that employers/customers desperately need.

THIS IS COMMON SENSE

1. There is always a NO VACANCY sign, yet people always get hired. So why not you?

2. You are a CEO of an enterprise. You work for yourself. The buck stops at your desk.

3. You are the ONLY person capable of limiting you and

influencing your happiness and success. You create your own circumstances.

4. Whatever your circumstance, someone else has gone through similar situations and has made a success of it. So why not you?

5. As your own CEO you are responsible for making profit.

6. To make profit you must engage in the problem solving equation.

ACTION EXERCISES

1. Write down a list of every person or situation you blame for your circumstances and results. After you've done that, cross out each name or item on your list and then write the words 'I am responsible for my circumstances and results.' Say it aloud to yourself.

2. Write down your goals for yourself as an enterprise.

3. Write down steps you can start to take from today to engage in the problem solving equation and earn rewards for yourself. Begin today to take action on the steps you've written.

Chapter Two

PEOPLE PAY FOR SOLUTIONS, NOT NECESSARILY YOUR DEGREES

When the beat of the drum changes, so must the steps to the dance.

- African proverb

At an interview, a candidate was asked how she could apply the knowledge from her course of study at university to the position she had applied for. She went into definitions of what the course was about but could not relate it to the position she had applied for. She could not show any usable knowledge or skill she had acquired from her course of study that would be relevant to the position. As you may have guessed, she was not given the job.

On the other hand, if you are able to bamboozle your way into a job with your certificates, the need to deliver on the expectations generated by your qualifications becomes important. Where the certified person cannot deliver on expectations based on actual usable skills, it usually leads to frustration and disappointment. Eventually, such people will be shown the way out by the employers. Omatseye's story illustrates this all too common situation vividly.

Omatseye's very numerous certificates and paper credentials were certainly impressive. In the ICT sector in Nigeria at the beginning of the millennium, when ICT was just beginning to touch lives and impact on the Nigerian economy, very few people had the collection of certificates in ICT proficiency that Omatseye had under his belt. Not many practitioners in the industry had actual technical experience, and so trainings, technical classes and professional examinations were the primary measure of acceptable proficiency. Omatseye's paper qualifications were enough to give him a pass practically anywhere in the ICT sector. With over ten such certificates in aspects of ICT ranging from Security to Voice Networks, Omatseye came fully loaded, or so it seemed.

Omatseye practically got a red carpet welcome into the organisation. We were pleased and thought ourselves lucky to have this 'whiz kid' in our organisation. Our expectations of this 'expert' were very high.

Omatseye's first test came when we got an IT security job with a bank and we quickly deployed our engineer to implement the solution. At first, we got excuses of all sorts from Omatseye as to how long it would take to conclude the project — we had already committed to a timeline and the customer expected us to have the job completed possibly before the agreed deadline. We conceded to Omatseye even though we knew it could be completed much earlier. Then came the shoddy work and poor work ethic, and the displayed lack of understanding of even the simplest ICT principles.

Omatseye would come up with different theories regarding what the problem could be, but each of these made little or no sense technically. At some point, he would make changes to the design and not document them appropriately, and this had a major negative impact on the customer.

The straw that broke the camel's back came when the customer insisted that Omatseye be withdrawn from his project or it would be cancelled. The customer's reason: Omatseye had no understanding of what he was to deliver; a job which was considered simple enough for any competent engineer with basic knowledge of ICT principles.

We had to withdraw Omatseye from the project, and he was replaced with a new engineer with fewer years in the industry and no certification. Within two weeks the customer gave us very good feedback regarding this new engineer. The customer stated that this new engineer demonstrated superior knowledge of ICT principles and was willing to consider situations from various angles and connect the dots before deciding on a course of action.

The project that had taken Omatseye over six months and resulted in no headway was completed and signed off within one month by a new engineer with no certification and less than half the number of years in practice that Omatseye had. Needless to say, the company had suffered reputational damage and erosion of margin due to cost overrun as a result of the various delays.

Omatseye was assigned two more projects, with the same outcomes and customer feedback: he was never able to complete a project and every customer said he lacked proper understanding of the fundamentals of ICT principles. He submitted his resignation less than two years after he was recruited.

About two years after Omatseye's resignation, I came across his curriculum vitae at an organisation where he had applied for a job. I was shocked at how glowingly he'd described his time at our company — the complexity of the project he'd handled and how well he'd tackled the challenges, and how he'd delivered the project within budget and on time. I was impressed with the CV and would have been interested in this engineer — the only difference was that by then I knew better. And by the way, Omatseye had gone on to acquire four more professional certifications since after leaving our employment.

In a nutshell, Omatseye had managed to obtain several certificates without understanding the very basic principles of the areas of knowledge they certified him as an expert in. He did not have the accompanying usable skills to complement his certification. The certificates got him a foot in the door but were not enough to earn him a permanent position in the organisation.

Certificates are good, but you must have usable skills. Employers and customers need people with the skills to provide usable solutions. It's the practical application of the knowledge you have that will create the solutions. Usable skills are preferred to certificates with no usable skills.

A while back we conducted a training session for an organisation. As is our normal procedure we had a needs analysis meeting with the president of the company. During the course of our discussion he told us about a particular staff member who had only a diploma but was more skilled and knowledgeable than most people with higher academic qualifications when it came to practical solutions. Given the value this staff member was providing, the president specifically created a special department for him to head. To the leader of the organisation, this individual was worth more to the company than most staff with "360 degrees" in the industry. This staff had what he needed —usable skills.

You may have gone to university to get a degree, but with the level of increase in information, expertise and demand for new skills to solve problems at higher performance levels; can you say you have the required expertise? Can you say with certainty that you have the skills to solve problems for an employer/customer? To be recruited for a job, you must have the ability to render value in excess of what it costs to pay for your service. A job is an opportunity to contribute value to an employer/customer in excess of your cost.

Your education, knowledge, skills and experience are all

investments in your ability to contribute value for which you can be paid by employers/customers. However, like any other investment, their worth cannot be definite and absolute. Considering the current alarming rate at which information and technology is becoming outdated and obsolete, you have to be on a continual self-upgrade program to solve today's problems and add value.

Once you have acquired any knowledge, skill or experience it becomes part of your past. No employer in the marketplace has any obligation to pay you for your past skill and experience, unless he or she can use your skill to produce a product or deliver a service that people are ready to pay for today. Simply put, employers/customers are interested in your future and your ability to contribute value to their organization on an ongoing basis. They do not necessarily pay for your degrees; they pay for your ability to use your degree and skills to provide solutions and add value.

THE RIGHT SOLUTION GETS ATTENTION

It was one of those days when one had to make a sales presentation to a client to sell the latest and best technology solution that we were sure was going to revolutionize the way the client worked. Everything was set: the PowerPoint presentations and the sales pitch had been well-prepared and rehearsed to near perfection. The customer had been appropriately qualified —they had a need for the solution, and the means to purchase it.

It was, however, a disappointment when after a brilliant sales pitch, the managing director of the company politely but firmly stated that they had a system in place which, while not meeting their needs exactly, simply needed to be optimized rather than replaced.

While packing up the presentation equipment and thanking them for their time, the entire management suddenly rushed out of the building. A power outage had occurred. This affected the entire building and, more importantly, their database storage (which is sensitive to sudden power losses). The management team was visibly shaken and upset as this had happened a while back and had cost them quite a huge sum to rectify.

Genuinely concerned about their challenge, we proceeded to ask them what the real issues were as they perceived them, and what the facts were. In the process we were able to decipher what some of the root causes were, and we proffered solutions that would not only forestall future data losses but would allow them better manage their power consumption and distribution.

Even though our sales appointment was not for power solution and we were not certified power experts, they called for our help to discuss these solutions in greater depth with the team as this was the number one challenge the establishment was facing at the time. This opened an instant door of opportunity beyond even the power situation. The initial solution we had made a presentation for was not accepted —a 'no vacancy' sign was placed on it —but the company had a vacancy for a solution provider for their problem of power and power management, which had a greater impact on their business.

Here is another interesting story:

In 1869 Thomas Edison moved from Boston to New York, friendless and in debt on account of the expenses of his experiment. For several weeks, he wandered about the town with actual hunger staring him in the face. It was

a time of great financial excitement, and with that strange quality of Fortunism, which seems to be his chief characteristic, he entered the establishment of the Law Gold Reporting Company just as their entire plant had shut down on account of an accident in the machinery that could not be located. The heads of the firm were anxious and excited to the last degree, and a crowd of the Wall Street fraternity waited about for the news which came not. The shabby stranger put his finger on the difficulty at once, and was given lucrative employment.[1]

The earlier story happened in the year 2014 in Nigeria while Edison's story happened in the United States in 1869 during the Industrial Revolution. Even with over a century and half between both stories, the interest of employers/customers has not changed —they remain interested in the right solutions.

While talking with a certain business owner about what qualities he would be looking for in a potential employee, he said: "If the person can show me how they can help me generate more business and increase my company's profitability, I will hire them immediately." You have to understand this: employers/customers are interested only in people that can give them the results they desire. They will be interested in you if you can show how you will help them meet their targets and achieve their goals.

IT'S NOT AN ENTITLEMENT

We encounter people on a regular basis who believe that they are entitled to jobs simply because they have attended university and obtained a degree. They think the government owes them a job. When they get a job they feel their employers owe them for employing them, and they complain incessantly based on their belief that they deserve more. However, when asked what solutions or value they have to offer to earn a job, a raise or a promotion, they become tongue-tied.

A young woman was expressing her grievance towards someone who she'd thought was in a position to help her but had failed to do so. What was her story? She had walked up to her would-be helper and told her she needed a job. Her would-be helper then asked her, "What can you do?" She began giving details about her degree. The woman interrupted her and asked again, "What can you do?" She could not identify what she could do specifically. Finally, the would-be helper suggested a few things the young woman could work on, but she was not interested in any suggestions. She was only interested in the woman offering her a job — any job.

At various times, while carrying out recruitment exercises for clients, we have come across individuals with the 'you owe me' mindset. One of the best questions to ask them is 'Why should you be given this job?' Another question frequently asked is 'What solution or value are you bringing to this organization?' Some have no clue what the company they have applied to is about and so do not know exactly what 'value' means to that organization. Others have nothing in particular to offer the company so they emphasize the degree(s) they have obtained. Another group believes they deserve the job because they are 'nice' people. Some candidates simply plan to show up and work hard. Others just need a place to earn their daily keep or make money, and appear to be begging for a job without offering any form of value.

We need to break this news to you: the era of jobs and job security is fast slipping away. No one is entitled to a job anymore. It is no longer possible to get and keep a job, or to get promoted and increase your income by just showing up at the office. Ironically, there are always jobs to be done, or rather, problems to be solved. For you to be the person for the job, you need to stand out. What makes you outstanding is being a solution provider that delivers results that people or organizations need. Here's a story to illustrate this point.

Stephanie was different. First, she was a female in an industry dominated by men. More importantly, though, she was different because she had a notebook she carried everywhere. In her notebook, she wrote instructions given to her, design concepts and solution architecture. But of more interest is what else she writes in her notebook: opportunities and ways to make situations better, and possible cost reduction areas for the company while increasing quality output.

Stephanie was a junior engineer. As was often the case in the organization where she worked, engineers were assigned projects to execute with the supervising project manager. Even in very complex ICT solutions, Stephanie always looked out for ways to improve on delivery. While other engineers concentrated on delivering good quality projects on time and within budget, Stephanie was concerned with delivering the very best quality project in the most optimal way while extracting a smile from the customer. She usually ended up creating another business opportunity with a client before she concluded an existing project. Before long, everyone wanted Stephanie on their team. She was always the first choice, even ahead of more senior engineers, and it was not uncommon to have teams squabble over her.

One day, the company had Evelyn attend a pre-project negotiation meeting so she could observe. During the negotiation process, however, Stephanie noticed a major error in an assumption her company had made. The assumption was on the client's facility on which the design of the solution was based. The error she noticed meant the design could not be executed with the present state of the client's facility. She carefully slipped a note to the Managing Director who was excited and ready to sign the agreement, bringing his attention to this error.

The Managing Director and his team of negotiators had to leave the negotiation table to verify this new information, and it was found that her observation was right. Even though the team was not happy that the deal could not be closed that day as this discovery entailed a major overhaul of the design, they were nonetheless glad that this flaw was detected before the deal was signed. It would have cost the company a lot to rectify this issue, and if they had chosen not to face the problem as a result of their design assumption, they would have suffered major reputational damage. Stephanie saved the company the needless cost and reputational damage. The entire management team took note of her from that day and this positioned her for opportunities to rise faster within the organization.

Whether in a good or bad economy, there are always challenges to be addressed and customers' needs to be met. People are always looking for solutions to problems. Employers/customers are always willing to pay someone who can provide the solution they need. It is therefore amazing that people search for jobs without giving some thought to what solutions they have to offer. They assume that the university degree they have obtained entitles them to a job. Well, it does not. Your certificate is only supposed to give you a foot in the door. The value you can bring via the solutions you provide is what gets you the job, the promotion and more rewards.

THINK VALUE FIRST

It is imperative that you think with the mindset of an entrepreneur. An entrepreneur is a person who solves problems for people at a profit. Providing solutions always comes first, and then the rewards or profits follow.

Being an entrepreneur is not just about trying to make money. It is about recognizing opportunities for solving problems, creating value, understanding and tapping into the customers' Willingness to Pay (WTP), and appropriating the value. If you've been looking for the secret to making your millions, here it is: solve other people's problems; understand and tap into their Willingness to Pay and they will pay you for it. Solve the challenge of an organization, or a whole lot of people, and they will contribute to making you a millionaire, or even a billionaire. The more people you help with your solution, the richer you become. Just to illustrate, if you wash somebody's dirty car, you've provided a solution and the person pays you. If you wash a few more cars, you've provided a solution to more people, so you earn more money. If you then go ahead to set up a system where at different locations you hire people to wash cars for lots of other people, you will be providing a solution to a lot of people, and you get to earn lots of money.

Think about it; when you have a challenge what do you do? You go to someone who can fix the problem for you. If your challenge is troublesome enough, you will probably pay the person for their solution. For example, if your car breaks down, you pay a mechanic to fix it. If you need help with washing your dirty clothes, you pay for laundry service. If you need help preparing food, you pay a cook. If the sink starts to leak or gets clogged, you pay a plumber to fix it. If your television develops a problem, you pay a technician to fix it. For everything you buy or pay for, someone helps you with a solution.

Every job and business is all about solutions. Just as you pay to get solutions, so do employers/customers pay to have their problems solved. Organizations pay people to be managing directors, chief operation officers, chief financial officers, regional managers, project managers, business development executives, sales executives, brand managers, marketing executives, customer relations officers etc. to provide them with the best solutions. No matter what title is assigned to the individual or position, the job is simply about being the solution to a particular challenge for the organization. The compensation and perks are based on the value the individual creates and the peculiar type of problem he or she solves.

BE KNOWN

If you must be known as a solution provider, you have to develop the habit of noting problems, coming up with solutions for them and becoming the provider of that solution. Find a way to help employers/customers lower costs, save money, save time, make more sales, increase productivity, hire better talent, reduce turnover, speed up a process, eliminate redundancy, keep existing customers, attract new customers, learn faster, or any one of many other things that would bring value to them. If you can do this, there will always be a vacancy for you. There is always a vacancy in organizations, and in the mind of customers,

for anyone with the relevant solution they need. It doesn't matter whether you are a fresh graduate in the market looking for a job, or presently employed but want to change jobs, or want a raise in your pay, or want to start a business. If you can solve an employer's or customer's problem, yes, there is a vacancy for you.

THIS IS COMMON SENSE

1. People have problems.

2. They need somebody to make the problems go away.

3. They are usually willing to pay for a solution if they see the value in it or if it is important enough to them.

4. Every successful product or service is a solution to a problem.

5. If you have a problem solver mindset, you seek these problems and provide solutions to them.

6. If you solve these problems and appropriate the value for the solution you create, you get rewarded. So why not become a problem solver?

ACTION EXERCISES

1. Starting right now, write down a list of problems that you have noticed your employer/customer facing and that you know they are willing to pay to get solved.

2. Write down possible solutions you can provide to each of these problems. Think through, research and then offer these solutions to them.

3. Write down a list of benefits they would get if you solve the

problem.

NOTES

[1]Orison Swett Marden, *How They Succeeded: Life Stories of Successful Men and Women Told by Themselves* (Boston: Lothorp, Lee and Shepard) 1901

Chapter Three

THE ULTIMATE ADVANTAGE

Money, if you use it, comes to an end; learning, if you use it, increases.

- Swahili proverb

Not long ago, a college student sent out a thirty-nine point questionnaire to all the presidents of fortune 500 companies. Eighty-three of those presidents completed the questionnaire and sent it back. This is an extraordinary number of responses from such a busy group of people.

The student went through the questionnaires to find out what these business leaders considered to be the reasons for their success. Perhaps the most common piece of advice from these top people, repeated over and over again, was, "Never stop learning and getting better." [2]

Some people stop learning after they graduate from university. They feel they have read enough books and passed examinations, and so they are finished with education. They have this idea that what they have learned thus far is all they need to succeed. This is an erroneous idea held by most people, at least subconsciously. It is a self-sabotaging idea. It keeps many people from providing relevant solutions that employers/customers would willingly pay more for.

The fact that you have completed your formal education doesn't mean that your education is over. Your university education is supposed to open your mind so you get into the learning mode and become a learner for life. You can only be prepared to seize opportunities through continuous learning.

Christopher Morley posits: "There are three ingredients to the good life: learning, earning, and yearning." This clearly highlights a principle that gets you paid more. There is always a gap between what you currently earn and what you really desire to earn. For some people this gap exists only because they have stopped stretching their problem solving muscle —their mind. This gap exists because they have not improved themselves beyond their present abilities or taken advantage of their capabilities.

IF YOU STOP STRETCHING YOU CUT YOUR EARNINGS

On the campus of the Obafemi Awolowo University, arranged in a neat row at the Student Union Building were the typists. Each of them had his/her well-worn but reliable typewriter. Business was always best towards the end of the second semester, when final year students submitted their theses or projects. A certain woman by the Student Union Building (SUB) stood out from the others —she was the fastest typist. She always had ready customers. Her typewriter was the old manual kind with the carriage return that moved from side to side. She was well-respected by the students, who clamoured to have her type their work because she could be counted upon to deliver in record time.

One day a new entrant into the typing business came on the scene with an electric typewriter. His shop was at the other end of the SUB. Unfortunately, he was not very good at using the electric

41

typewriter at first, and he ended up delaying students' theses and producing lower quality work compared with the woman at the SUB. He was not exactly on the students' recommendation list. The woman at the SUB was seen sometimes scoffing at the new entrant with his strange electric typewriter. She was very comfortable with the manual one and was not willing to let it go. Business was good, her client base was solid —she had more referrals than she could cope with. Students even begged to be kept on her wait list.

However, by the end of the first semester of the next session, the woman had lost most of her clients. The electric typist had learned to effectively operate his machine and his output was now faster and neater than what was obtainable from any manual typewriter. The woman, however, continued to scoff at the electric typist and believed this phenomenon was just a phase that would be gone by the end of the session. As far as she was concerned, she still had better customer service, since she had some references from what was left of her customers. To her, she had only lost the "bothersome" customers who always asked to be kept on her wait list —good riddance.

Fast forward two years and the woman no longer had any customer; she had to leave with her manual typewriter. Even the electric typist was becoming redundant by then as students had been presented with the option of computers. Even though computers were few, they were much more efficient. Corrections, which used to be such a nightmare to make (usually using Tipp-Ex), could now be made with a single click.

It took less than two years (from the time of this event) to have the SUB cleared of all manual typists, and less than four to replace all electric typewriters with computers. The woman was so good at what she did but her service became obsolete along with the old technology.

Ironically, there was an increase in demand for typing service, but she was used to an old technology and refused to learn and adapt to the new, which met the demand for the services required.

You need to continuously feed your mind with new information. If you stop stretching your mind, which is your problem-solving tool, you are limiting your ability, and ultimately your opportunity to earn more. If you are not investing in acquiring new knowledge and learning more desirable skills, know that you are sabotaging your efforts to earn more. You cannot earn higher by using the same skills you are currently being paid for. You do not get paid more for working harder with the knowledge you acquired long ago. This is because you can only keep getting the same level of results you've always gotten, and nothing more.

A popular saying goes thus: "The more you do of what you're doing, the more you'll get of what you are getting." It is insanity to keep doing more of what you're doing and expect a better result. You cannot perform better by using your current skills and knowledge. You cannot be given a responsibility you do not have the ability to handle; and if you do not handle more responsibilities and solve bigger problems you will not be paid more. This is because the bigger the problem you solve the higher an employer/customer will be willing to pay.

Think about this: the knowledge and skill level of an ordinary computer user and that of an organization's IT manager are not the same. The knowledge and skill level of a gatekeeper is not the same as that of a security technology management expert. The knowledge and skill level of an IT officer and an IT division manager are not the same. Without upgrading their knowledge and skills, the basic computer user, the gatekeeper and the IT officer cannot be paid more. They will only be paid to the extent to which their present level of knowledge and skill is rated by their employer/customer.

CHANGE YOUR RATINGS

A rating is the evaluation of something in terms of quality, quantity or a combination of both. If the problems you solve do not rate high in quality (high standard) or quantity (high numbers) then your ratings will definitely be poor. Also, if the problems you solve do not rate high in priority and need, your ratings will be low. This is because the more difficult and troublesome the problem, the higher the demand for the solution; and the higher the demand for the solution, the higher you get paid. You will rise in life to the height that employers/customers rate the problems you are capable of solving. Poor ratings from employers and customers equal low pay. Low pay means your solutions are not considered highly important or relevant.

Management consultant Tom Peters says that "Irrelevance comes from always doing the things you know how to do in the way you've always done them." This means that what used to be your best skills will not be good enough for growth to higher levels of performance that will get you paid more. You have to learn and practice something new and different to change your ratings. To do more or better you have to learn more. If you do not increase your ratings by learning more you will reach a level where you are no longer seen as competent enough to solve your employer's/customer's problems. At this point you will be operating at the level of incompetence, which makes your ratings very low. At this level you will not be given higher responsibility that will get you paid more. And if your skill and knowledge have lost much relevance to an employer, during a downsizing exercise you will be fired.

There is an explosion of technology and knowledge, and what used to be 'the best' knowledge and skill rapidly becomes 'not good enough' for employers/customers. To perform and deliver relevant solutions that will attract much higher pay, you need to learn more at a faster rate. The more you know the better you will be at solving problems. The better and faster you are at solving problems the more money employers/customers will be willing to pay you.

LEARN THE KEY SKILL

If you can think about this critically you will realize that the key skill you need to get is learning how to learn continually. Particular knowledge and skills can become obsolete with the passage of time, but learning how to learn continually will enable you transit quickly and seamlessly to current skills and knowledge that would be relevant at every given time. Developing a continual learning ability or habit is the best advantage you can give yourself. You learn, earn, and then yearn for more knowledge and skill. This is the success cycle for people who solve problems and rise to the top as high achievers.

The marketplace is continually evolving as the needs of customers change. Old knowledge and skills may not be able to solve current problems. Yesterday's best skills are no longer good enough to render the best services for today. People who are unable to quickly learn and make the change to modern and relevant technologies for more effective operations will lose their jobs and customers. If you are not continually learning and growing, the knowledge you have is actually diminishing. The person that will be seen as incompetent tomorrow is the person who stops learning today. The illiterate person is the person who is no longer learning, growing and increasing his value every single day. Eric Hoffer's epic quote sums it up: "In a time of drastic change it is the learners who inherit the future. The learned usually find themselves equipped to live in a world that no longer exists."

If your tools are outdated they cannot be the best tools to fix today's problems. If the only tool you have is a hammer, you will tend to see every problem as a nail. All problems are not 'nails', but since your outdated 'hammer' is all you have you will treat all problems as nails; and if the problem happens to be in the form of 'glass', instead of solving it you will shatter it and create more problems for your employer/customer.

Continual learners are never outdated. They stay young. Being young is about having a mind that keeps learning. It is the extent to which your mind absorbs new information to generate fresh ideas and better approaches to providing solutions. When you continuously learn you stay young and relevant because you are always updated.

HOW TO BECOME A CONTINUAL LEARNER

To keep yourself from becoming antiquated you need to understand that you are on a quest for knowledge, skills, new ideas and approaches to doing a better job or rendering the best service for your employer/customer. You have to develop a passion for learning. If you do, your earnings will never cease to grow. The growth of your earnings is dependent on how much relevant knowledge and skills you are able to acquire at a given time. You can always earn more if you take some time to learn more. Learning is profitable, so you have to be passionate about it and begin today to build a learning culture.

The best way to create a future where you earn more is to step out of the group of 'once and for all' learners and become a continual learner. Here are some simple steps you can take to become a continual learner.

- Adopt a growth mindset.

One thing that might be keeping you back from learning new things is the belief that you cannot. But neuroscience and psychology have shown this to be false. Our brains remain plastic and malleable well into old age, and it's possible to create new connections among neurons and learn new things even at age 70.

Stanford psychologist Carol Dweck discovered that people have one of two 'mindsets' —fixed or growth. Individuals with a fixed mindset believe that their intelligence and talents are innate and fixed. They don't think they can improve by working hard and applying effort. People with a growth mindset believe that with effort they can become top achievers. They believe that they can improve themselves through working hard to learn something new, and by practicing. To become a continual learner you need to embrace the growth mindset. You embrace the growth mindset by:

·   Focusing on learning and improving

·   Seeking challenges and trying new things that will require your mind to be stretched

·   Putting in more effort and persisting regardless of setbacks

·   Focusing on creating, applying and adjusting strategies to achieve your goal

- Change your impression of learning.

Learning doesn't have to be in a formal classroom setting. In fact, a great percentage of the useful information you have was picked up informally from your family, friends, colleagues, mentors and through the process of trial and error. To become a continual learner, drop the idea that you must sign up for a class to learn something.

Learning opportunities are all around you. Information is just a click away, thanks to the internet. Also, keep in mind that learning isn't confined to what's found in books or audio training programs — acquiring practical skill sets is a big part of it too.

- Set goals. What do you want to learn? Why do you need to learn it? When do you want to be done learning it? How will you go about learning it? Every year, set goals for yourself on skills and knowledge that you want to enhance and update, and those you want to acquire. Make sure your goals are SMART (Specific, Measurable, Achievable, Realistic and Time bound).

- Find your sources. Once you establish your learning goals, it's time to get sources. You can do an online search to see what information is available. You can go to the library and bookshops to see what you can find. Online retailers like Amazon provide e-book readers and software applications that make it quite convenient to carry your library around with you. If you're trying to learn a skill that will require special instruction, search for places or individuals that could offer that instruction and start checking them out.

- Learn to invest time. Be intentional about how you invest your time.

There are all sorts of spare moments that you can turn into learning opportunities —during your regular jog or workout, commuting, using the toilet, waiting in line or for a service. Research shows that you can get the equivalent of full-time university attendance by listening to audio books and training programs as you drive from place to place. With today's technology you can even load audio books and e-books onto your mobile phone and other devices.

Listen to an audio book during your commute instead of your favourite music playlist. You have to consciously make learning a priority if you are to effectively invest time in it.

- **Practice, practice, practice.** Don't just read or listen your way to knowledge. Try to find a way to put that knowledge to work providing solutions that are faster, better or more innovative. Remember, employers/customers will not pay you for what you have learned. They only pay for the problems you solve with what you have learned. And they will be willing to pay more if you are able to do more with whatever you learn.

THIS IS COMMON SENSE

1. Your knowledge and skills determine how much you are paid.
2. You limit your ability to earn more if your knowledge and skill rating is low in quantity and quality.
3. You cut your ability to earn more if your skill and knowledge loses relevance over time.
4. You can get your employer/customer to pay you more by learning more.

5. Your path to getting paid more as a problem solver is to invest time learning more. You can learn anything by simply reading books, listening to audio training programs, taking relevant classes and attending seminars.

6. You will keep earning more if you embrace the mindset of continual learning.

ACTION EXERCISES

1. Examine your current skill and knowledge level and compare it to that of someone earning what you would like to be paid.

2. Research and write down the level of skill you need to have in order to be paid the amount you desire.

3. Set a goal to acquire this level of skill and knowledge, and then write down the steps you will take to achieve it.

NOTES

[2]Brian Tracy, *The Psychology of Selling* (Nashville: Thomas Nelson) 2004

Chapter Four

BECOME A THINKER

What makes sense today may be madness tomorrow.

- Nigerian proverb

During the process of analyzing the training needs for a certain real estate firm, the managing director says about his staff, "Sometimes it's as though they don't think. I need them to begin thinking creatively and more strategically." In another organization in the oil and gas sector, the MD says out of exasperation, "I don't need people that have only physical muscle. What I need is mental energy. I need people who think, people who use their minds, people who work smart. That is what we need to grow this company."

No matter what kind of organization you work for, in today's world you are expected to apply a range of thinking skills in carrying out your job. You work by thinking. The more effectively you think and the better prepared you are mentally, the more productive and positive you'll be. Whatever it is that you do, the quality of thinking that goes into the delivery of your work will determine how effectively you are able to solve problems for an employer/customer. Your thinking skills will determine how successful you ultimately become.

David Schwartz asserts: "Where success is concerned, people are not measured in inches, or pounds, or college degrees, or family background; they are measured by the size of their thinking." Simply put, your thinking equals your result. The reverse is also true: your result equals your thinking. The level to which you are able to deliver the best solutions depends on your ability to think up the solutions in the first place; and your ability to think up these solutions determines your reward.

The greatest resource you have is your mind, your thinking tool. Consequently, one of the best investments you can make is to learn how to use this powerful tool to produce valuable solutions that employers/customers need. It is often said that Nigeria is blessed with abundant human and natural resources. However, on close observation, you will find that this statement is not entirely true. Nigeria as a nation is blessed with abundant natural resources and a lot of human beings. For human beings to transit into being human resources, their thinking capability and capacity need to be engaged and enlarged. This perhaps is one of the reasons why, since before Nigeria's independence in 1960, the whole world has been saying that Nigeria is full of potential. To date, over 55 years after independence, Nigeria is still described as a nation with potential —but this potential has never been actualized. We posit that for Nigeria as a nation and as a people to move to the level of actualizing our collective potential, we need to become a thinking nation.

FAULTY THINKING

Most people neglect the use of their minds to think and solve problems. This is an act of self-sabotage. Some people would do everything but think. They tend to believe there is no way to solve the problems they face. They are always confused, expecting others to do their thinking for them. I used to wonder why this was, until I got an answer from Henry Ford who explained that "Thinking is the hardest work there is, which is probably the reason why so few engage in it."

Thomas Edison points out that 85 percent of people would rather die than think. Another 10 percent of people do not know how to think effectively. But there is the five percent of real thinkers. Now, if you become a part of this five percent imagine the advantage you will have. You will become part of the few that are being sought after for their skills as problem solvers; and the rewards will be very gratifying.

People who are not part of the five percent engage in faulty thinking patterns. Effective thinking is indeed hard work, so instead of engaging in it most people engage in self-sabotaging thoughts that prevent them from thinking effectively. It is not to your advantage to be part of this group because you will not be able to produce solutions, or at best you will produce mediocre solutions. Your mind is a double-edged sword. If you fill it with the right thoughts it will lead you to the path of high productivity. But if you allow it to run wild or fill it with negative thoughts it will lead you to produce mediocre results or, worse still, nothing. In computing, GIGO is an acronym meaning Garbage In, Garbage Out. When it comes to the human mind, garbage in produces multiplied and enhanced garbage out.

Your mind produces results based on your inputs, so you cannot afford to accommodate faulty patterns of thinking. If you find yourself operating in any of the following ways, note that you are engaged in faulty thinking patterns:

- When your mind remains in a state of worry when faced with a problem.

- If you always feel overwhelmed and think you can't solve the problems that you are presented with.

- If you always think you will fail in your attempt to solve a problem.

- If you are always afraid when given the responsibility to think up a solution or if you think you are not creative and cannot

53

generate ideas.

- If you are too indifferent or lazy to get necessary information and facts with which to think accurately, and you rely on guesswork.

- If you constantly avoid work that needs any serious mental effort.

- If you come to conclusions too quickly, without considering the facts and context of the problem.

Faulty thinking patterns sabotage your solution generating mechanism —your mind.

Faulty thinking patterns are as a result of a negative perception and response to problems. Most people view problems as calamitous things to be avoided by all means. Most people, when they encounter a problem, react with panic or despair. For some south westerners in Nigeria, the reaction is usually *"Mo Gbe!"* which literally translates —"I am finished." This reaction is in itself a problem, and an often bigger one than the problem itself. Here are a few ways in which people react to problems:

- They refuse to acknowledge the problem, sometimes going into outright denial (possibly hoping the problem will disappear)

- They feel overwhelmed and give in to despair

- They ask 'why me?'

- They start a pity party

- They simply give up

- They take flight from the problem

- They make it someone else's problem

- They immediately start to fight the problem without much thought (reactive approach)

- They blame someone else and remain at that point

- They acknowledge the problem, seek the root cause and generate possible solutions (responsive approach)

For you to be able to solve any challenge in life you must first adopt the right perception of what a problem is. We need to understand that a problem is:

- The difference between where you are and where you want to be.

- The recognition that there is something better than the current situation.

- An opportunity to exercise your mental muscles.

- A chance to provide a remarkable solution that will make a positive impact.

- An opportunity to learn.

EFFECTIVE THINKING

The phrase "Yoi shina, yoi kangae" (meaning "good thinking, good product") is a line from a popular Toyota advert from many years back. This Toyota slogan states a very important fact: you can only produce a good product when you engage in effective thinking. This is thinking focused on generating solutions to problems. Good thinking can change your life. It can solve problems, generate revenue and create opportunities. It can take you to a whole new level, personally and professionally.

According to Microsoft Encarta, "thinking involves the mental manipulation of information for the purpose of reasoning, solving problems, making decisions and judgments, or simply imagining." This means intentional thought, based on information, to produce a desired result. When faced with problems, people often worry instead of applying their minds intentionally to come up with solutions. Some people believe that worrying is some kind of thinking. Indeed it is, but it is not solution-oriented thinking. It is just imagining possible negative outcomes and feeling agitated because you presently cannot see a solution to the problem you face.

Effective thinking is not worrying. The kind of thinking that produces desirable results has nothing to do with worrying. Effective thinking is known as critical thinking. Diane Halpern, an award-winning professor of psychology, offers this definition in her seminal book, *Thought and Knowledge*: "Critical thinking is the use of those cognitive skills or strategies that increase the probability of a desirable outcome. It is used to describe thinking that is purposeful, reasoned, and goal-directed —the kind of thinking involved in solving problems, formulating inferences, calculating likelihoods, and making decisions... It's the kind of thinking that makes desirable outcomes more likely." This is 'intentional' thinking. This kind of thinking focuses on generating solutions to problems. It is methodical thinking that requires self-discipline. People who think effectively approach thinking in this manner.

CHANGE YOUR THINKING ALTITUDE

The five percent of real thinkers approach thinking intentionally using a set of techniques. In most cases, the reason people engage in self-sabotaging thought patterns is that they have not learned the approaches, skills and techniques that will help them think through problems. Ignorance of effective approaches to solving problems can be crippling, resulting in faulty or low-level thinking. Of course, this will not produce desirable results.

You have to improve your thinking ability so that you can think at a higher level. Only by thinking at a higher level can you solve problems. Doing this means making the necessary effort to build your mind to think effectively.

EXERCISE YOUR MIND

Becoming an expert in your field and continually upgrading your skill is like working on your physical fitness. If you stop exercising for any period of time, your fitness does not remain at the same level. Your body and muscles will become softer and weaker. You will lose your strength, flexibility and stamina. In order to maintain them, you must keep working at it every week, every month and every year.

Many people are aware that physical fitness is important, and some people allocate time to exercise, but what about mind fitness? How many people allocate time to exercising their minds? Not many, I'm afraid. But the few who do will far surpass others when it comes to solving problems for employers/customers.

Good thinkers are always in demand. Employers/customers are always looking for the best minds that can provide them with solutions, so just as you should allocate time for physical exercise you should do the same for mind exercise. This way you will improve the fitness of your mind and place yourself in a position of high demand.

A very important aspect to exercising your mind is feeding it with lots of good and relevant information. You can do this by reading and listening to valuable material every day. Read books and articles, listen to audio programs and attend seminars. If you want to solve a problem in a particular area make sure you feed your mind with information about that area. For instance, if you want to develop a good marketing strategy, you can start by feeding your mind with the best marketing information available. Feeding your mind with good input gets it activated. It gets the thinking process started.

The other very important aspect to exercising the mind is engaging it to solve problems. To make the exercise useful, use it to handle real problems you face. Make a list of problems you would like to solve for an employer/customer. You can also include personal problems. Just make sure you list real problems that you are facing. After making your list, choose a problem that you need to solve. You will be more enthusiastic to practice if you know that you need the solution. The more you need the solution, the more motivated you will be.

After you pick a problem, you should pick a thinking technique to solve it with. You can learn some techniques from books like Michael Michalko's *Thinkertoys*, Scott Thorpe's *How to Think Like Einstein,* James Higgins's *101 Creative Problem Solving Techniques* and John C. Maxwell's *How Successful People Think*. Practice intentionally. Use these techniques to the best of your ability. You can only increase your capacity if you push yourself slightly beyond your current limit. So try your best with the techniques you choose and push yourself a bit more. Let your mind muscles get some training. Also, make sure you write down the ideas you generate so you don't forget them. After your exercise you can then choose some of your ideas and put them into practice.

Thinking Techniques

To become a more effective thinker you must learn effective thinking skills and techniques with which to approach and solve problems. Here are three simple prevalent techniques you can use.

-Mindstorming

Mindstorming is a creative problem solving methodology often called 'The 20-Idea Method'. You start by defining your goal or problem as a question. For example, 'How do I increase my income by 30 percent over the next 12 months?' Then discipline yourself to write down at least 20 answers to the question. Out of your 20 answers, select one from your list and take immediate action on it. You will be amazed at the quality and quantity of ideas you generate by doing this on a regular basis.

- The Six Universal Questions

Asking these questions will guide you towards answers that lead to solutions. These questions are Why? Where? When? Who? What? and How? For example:

Why is it necessary?

Where should it be done?

When should it be done?

Who should do it?

What should be done?

How should it be done?

- Five Whys

Five Whys refers to the practice of asking, five times, why the problem exists, in order to get to its root cause. Ask 'Why' a problem is occurring, and then ask 'Why' four more times. Here is an example:

1. Why am I unemployed?

   Answer: No one wants to hire me.

2. Why won't anyone hire me?

   Answer: I don't meet their requirements.

3. Why don't I meet their requirements?

   Answer: I don't have the necessary skills.

4. Why don't I have the necessary skills?

   Answer: I have not acquired them.

5. Why have I not acquired them?

   Answer: I have not invested in learning.

Investing in self-development to acquire relevant skills solves the problem.

These are just a few of the many structured critical thinking skills and techniques that can be applied to solving a variety of problems.

You must invest conscious effort to learn and use various thinking skills and techniques if you are to become a thinker that is highly sought after for solutions. You must recognize your mind as your most important asset. It is the asset that solves problems for employers/customers. It is your greatest capital for exchange in the marketplace. It cannot be affected by economic depression or recession. If consistently cultivated and managed it will produce solutions that will earn you great rewards. Think about this.

THIS IS COMMON SENSE

1. Every solution is provided through the use of your greatest resource —your mind.

2. If you can think to solve problems, your opportunities become limitless. You will be in constant demand.

3. Engaging in faulty thinking sabotages your ability to solve problems for an employer/customer.

4. You have to engage in effective thinking. This will enable you solve problems for employers/customers.

5. To enhance your ability to think effectively you have to continuously exercise your mind by feeding it relevant information and intentionally engaging it to solve problems.

6. To help give focus and method to your thinking, use effective thinking skills and techniques.

ACTION EXERCISES

1. Write down the opportunities you will enjoy if you solve the problems facing an employer/customer.

2. Buy at least one book in a year that will teach you usable skills and techniques to enhance your ability to think and solve problems.

3. Write down real problems your employer/customer needs to solve and apply your mind to solving them, using some of the skills and techniques in this chapter.

Chapter Five

BECOME A GENIUS

The lizard that jumped from the high iroko tree said he would praise himself if no one else would.

- **Nigerian proverb**

Becoming a genius sets you apart. There are geniuses in various fields of endeavour, and you can become one too if you so choose. There is a common misconception that one is either born a genius or not. But nobody has any proof of this. We assume this to be true because we have heard it so many times.

Dr. Benjamin Solomon Carson Snr., one of the brightest minds in the field of neurosurgery, credited with being the first surgeon to separate conjoined twins joined at the head (occipital craniopagus twins), was considered so dumb by his classmates and teachers in elementary school that he was the object of ridicule. He developed a violent temper as a result of his low self-esteem. This persisted until his mother got him and his brother to visit the library to read books, limiting their TV time to a select program per week.

They were required to read two books per week and submit written reports on each of them to their mother. Carson went from being a "dullard" to being the youngest director of paediatric neurosurgery at Johns Hopkins University at the age of 33. Also, he was awarded 38 honorary degrees and was conferred with the Ford's Theatre Lincoln Medal and the Presidential Medal of Freedom, the U.S.'s highest civilian honours, in February 2008.

Thomas Edison's teachers had said he was "too stupid to learn anything." The tutor of Warren Buffet, one of the greatest investors of our time, was said to have advised his parents to find him a career unrelated to investments because he was not qualified. But the world has come to know these men as geniuses. Think about that.

Given the observable facts, we have come to know that being a genius is not about having an extraordinarily high I.Q., or even about being smart. Dr. Alfred Barrios explains that

> […] if you look at the lives of the world's greatest geniuses like Edison, Socrates, DaVinci, Shakespeare, Einstein, you will discover they all had (certain) personality characteristics in common. […] It makes no difference how old you are, how much education you have, or what you have accomplished to date. Adopting these personality characteristics enables you to operate on a genius level.

Becoming a genius is about mastering certain principles and conducts, which the world's geniuses adopt, to produce genius solutions in a chosen field. It does not necessarily have anything to do with your IQ, or with being born a genius. Surprisingly, anyone can learn these principles and develop these traits. Let's consider some of them.

DRIVE

Geniuses have a strong desire to work hard and long. They are not lethargic. They have high energy. They're willing to give all they've got to a project. Thomas Edison was renowned for his drive. He often worked 18 hours a day, surviving on catnaps and four to five hours of sleep per night.

You will have to push yourself hard when solving problems, whether on your job or with your personal goals.

Focusing on your future success strengthens your drive. Think about the rewards that you will enjoy when you succeed. Think about the impact you will make. Keep pushing hard at the problem and you will unravel a unique solution.

COURAGE

A defining characteristic of a genius is the ability to act in spite of fear. The path of a genius is paved with insecurities, misunderstanding, rejection, ridicule and, in some cases, outright hostility. Nelson Mandela shares that he "learned that courage was not the absence of fear, but the triumph over it. The brave man is not he who does not feel afraid, but he who conquers that fear."

It takes courage to solve problems. It takes courage to do things others consider impossible. Muhtar Bakare gave up his position as a bank executive in Nigeria to start an independent publishing house. Many must have thought this was foolhardy. But today his company, Kachifo Limited, popularly known as Farafina, is a household name, publishing works of renowned authors such as Chimamanda Ngozi Adichie, Ngugi wa Thiong'o and Eghosa Imasuen. Stop worrying about what people will think if you're different. As Muhammad Ali said, "He who is not courageous enough to take risks will accomplish nothing in life." It takes courage to solve problems. So feel the fear but go ahead. Like the Nike slogan says, 'Just do it.'

CLARITY OF VISION AND COMMITMENT TO GOALS

Geniuses know what they want and go after it. Geniuses formulate very clear and precise inner pictures of what they want to accomplish, how they will do it, and what success they intend to achieve. You need to get control of your life and focus on a goal.

Set definite goals on problems you want to solve. Immerse 100 percent of yourself into achieving it. Have something specific to accomplish each day that takes you closer to the goal. Orison Swett Marden said, "All who have accomplished great things have had a great aim, have fixed their gaze on a goal which was high, one which sometimes seemed impossible." A good example is the clarity of vision and commitment to goals as demonstrated by Fola Adeola and Tayo Aderiokun, the founders of Guaranty Trust Bank Plc. in Nigeria. Their vision was to create the utmost in customer service and to be synonymous with innovation in the banking sector. You have to commit yourself to higher goals that solve problems for employers/customers. Be clear about it, commit to it and stay focused until you achieve it.

KNOWLEDGE

The genius neurosurgeon, Ben Carson, makes a point in saying that "Knowledge is the key that unlocks all the doors. You can be green-skinned with yellow polka dots and come from Mars, but if you have knowledge that people need instead of beating you, they'll beat a path to your door." Geniuses continually accumulate information. They spend time gathering enough information on problems they want to solve. Be sure to read and ask questions from people who know. Never go to sleep at night without having learned at least one new thing each day.

With the knowledge explosion in today's world, there is a limitless amount of information available to you in whatever field. You can learn a lot by reading. Reading activates your mind. By reading, you gain information that helps your mind connect dots and come up with innovative and creative solutions to problems.

HONESTY

Geniuses are frank, forthright and honest. Unlike most people, they take decisive action when confronted with hard facts. They acknowledge when something is not working and change track.

You have to face brutal reality. Be willing to admit when you make a blunder, and make the necessary changes needed to achieve your goal. When something is not working, don't delude yourself; accept that it's simply not working and try to find an alternative.

OPTIMISM AND FAITH

"Optimism is a strategy for making a better future. Because unless you believe that the future can be better, you are unlikely to step up and take responsibility for making it so." These are the words of Noam Chomsky. Geniuses are optimistic. They approach problems believing that a brilliant solution can and will be found. They have confidence that a breakthrough discovery will be made.

Geniuses never dwell on doubts. They have faith in themselves and in their ability to achieve their goals. Geniuses are possibility thinkers. They believe even when it is beyond the power of reason to believe. You need to deliberately focus your mind on something good coming up. You need to be positively minded that a solution can be found; and you need to believe you have the ability to find the solution. If you do not believe, you have failed before you even start.

KEEP AN OPEN MIND

Geniuses try to understand the facts of a situation before they judge. They evaluate things with an open mind. They spend time considering all possible ways of approaching or solving a problem. You must be unprejudiced and learn to let go of narrow-minded thinking. You must be willing to test assumptions because as the saying goes, 'assumption is the lowest form of intelligence'.

Be willing to change your mind whenever you get more or better information; and also be willing to test your information for veracity. Orville and Wilbur Wright went ahead to invent the airplane despite the information that man cannot fly. Think about that. They questioned that information and today we can fly. Never be quick to say 'it's impossible.' You might only need new information to do the seemingly impossible, because even the word impossible, re-evaluated, means '**I'm possible**'.

ENTHUSIASM

Geniuses are excited about what they do. They have an infectious enthusiasm that encourages others to cooperate with them. You have to be really excited, believing that things will turn out well, and you will solve whatever problem you have been presented with.

Your level of enthusiasm determines the amount of effort you put into your goal, and the extent to which others will cooperate with you.

TAKING CHANCES

Geniuses are willing to take chances. They are not afraid of failure. Failing is getting feedback to self-correct, after which you can begin again, more intelligently. You won't be afraid to take chances once you realize that failure is part of the process of achieving success.

Succeeding often comes from learning from your mistakes. When you work towards achieving any goal you are taking a chance that you might fail. But the only way to succeed is to take a chance. The individual who goes farthest is generally the one who is willing to do and dare.

DYNAMIC ACTION

Geniuses don't sit around waiting for something good to happen. They make it happen. They take action. Action is not an option for the genius. It's a vital part of the problem solving formula. Thomas Edison constantly took action on his ideas, which is why he patented more than 1000 inventions. His taking action on his idea is the reason we have the incandescent light bulb we all use today.

You have to take action to make it happen. Pablo Picasso's summation is that "Action is the foundational key to all success." All geniuses take action towards achieving their goals. As an act of genius you must take consistent action to provide valuable solutions for employers/customers. You must take action to achieve your desired goals.

SPIRIT OF ENTERPRISE

Geniuses are opportunity seekers —they look for problems and develop solutions. They take on assignments that nobody wants to touch. They tread unknown paths.

You have to be willing to take on jobs others won't touch. Never be afraid to try the unknown. From light bulbs to airplanes, computers, the internet, satellites, iPads, smart phones etc., all are as a result of the spirit of enterprise of geniuses. You have to develop the knack for taking on daring new projects.

EFFECTIVE COMMUNICATION

Geniuses are able to effectively get their ideas across to others. They are able to communicate the value of their ideas and how they work. A brilliant example of this was the way Steve Jobs used the full power of his mystique, his environment and his technology, while launching Apple's products, to show people how the company's latest innovations would change the world.

You need to learn how to effectively communicate your ideas. Use every opportunity to practice explaining your ideas to others. Learning the art of effective communication enables you sell the value you provide.

PERFECTIONISM

Geniuses cannot tolerate mediocrity, particularly in themselves. They constantly push themselves to the greatest heights of excellence. Steve Jobs of Apple was known to rehearse his presentations to the point of perfection. He wanted the design of the touch buttons on the iPad to look so good that one would want to lick them.

Never be easily satisfied with yourself. Be your own taskmaster. Be the one to redefine what excellent work is. There is a place called 'better', just beyond the island called 'best.'

A SENSE OF HUMOUR

Geniuses are able to laugh at their failures. Take your work seriously, but learn to take yourself lightly. Be willing to laugh at your own expense. A sense of humour is good for creativity. Don't take offense when the joke is on you.

Be willing to laugh at your own mistakes and seeming failures. Humour flushes out stress. It helps your body to generate more positive energy to persist in your search for solutions. Learn to laugh at your failures and try again. Just ask yourself, what would I do differently?

ADAPTABILITY

Geniuses have the mental fluidity to think swiftly, generate new ideas and consider alternatives. Openness to change is one of the defining traits of a genius. In Adaptability: The Art of Winning in an Age of Uncertainty, Max McKeown says, "All failure is failure to adapt, and all success is successful adaptation."

You have to resist the urge to do things the same old way. Be willing to consider new options. Learn to be flexible. Being flexible enables you to adapt to changing circumstances readily.

CURIOSITY

Geniuses have the most curious minds. They are insatiable, always questioning, always trying to learn something new. An inquisitive, curious mind will help you seek out new information. Don't be afraid to admit you don't know it all. Always ask questions about things you don't understand.

Every invention developed by geniuses is as a result of curiosity. They questioned the status quo and discovered new information that made the seeming impossible possible. A certain friend of mine, who we all consider a genius as he displays most of these qualities we've examined, never ceases to amaze people when he declares ignorance on a subject, without any pretension. He asks questions and absorbs knowledge, and is never ashamed to learn something new. Stay curious.

IMAGINATION

Everything ever designed, invented or created was first imagined before it was brought to reality through focused effort. Without imagination the solutions we have today would not exist.

Without imagination you are limited in your ability to solve problems. Using their imagination, geniuses think in new combinations, seeing things from a perspective different from anyone else's. Give yourself time each day to fantasize, like you did as a child. Your history is your past but your imagination is your future. Visualize unlimited possibilities. It is possible if you can imagine it.

KEEP WORKING

The period between beginning the move toward your goal and achieving it can be discouraging. But you must know that the process you go through is all part of learning and getting better. You are gaining knowledge and understanding of what doesn't work, so you eventually get to know what does work.

Geniuses embrace this process. They keep working on themselves and on their tasks and projects. They know that this makes them better. Geniuses don't give up or waste time brooding. They know that persistence is necessary for producing genius solutions. So just keeping working no matter what.

WORK YOUR GENIUS

Now you know some of the qualities that make a genius, and as you can see they are not about how high your IQ is. Your ability to develop and internalize these traits will enable you function at genius level to solve problems for employers/customers, and ultimately earn you great rewards. Make a habit of these characteristics and you will find yourself achieving more and being sought after as a solution provider.

THIS IS COMMON SENSE

1. Anyone can choose to become a genius.

2. Many people who were called dumb and stupid have become known today as geniuses.

3. Being a genius does not necessarily have to do with how high your IQ is.

4. Geniuses are not born; they are made.

5. Becoming a genius has to do with mastering certain principles and conducting yourself in particular ways.

6. If you adopt these principles and practice them continually until they become part of your personality, you will operate at genius level when you solve problems for employers and customers.

ACTION EXERCISES

1. Make a decision to become a genius at solving problems starting from today.

2. Invest time studying the principles highlighted in this chapter.

They will help you earn great rewards.

3. Write down the genius traits that you do not yet possess, and take action to consciously adopt them in your approach to solving problems on a daily basis.

Chapter Six

ATTITUDE COUNTS

The child who washes his hands clean gets to eat with the elders.

- **Nigerian proverb**

Attitude is the product of a mindset, a point of view about an idea, situation or person. This point of view can be positive or negative. Research shows that attitude includes three components: an affect (what you feel), cognition (what you think or believe) and behaviour (what you do). You are able to control these components through the choices you make. You choose how you want to feel. You choose what to believe. You also choose how you act.

Your attitude is your choice, whether it is positive or negative. This choice, as simple as it is, determines your future. It determines how you tackle problems and provide solutions. Your attitude is the way you approach life. It is your general mental tone and the outward expression of your thoughts and feelings.

A positive mental attitude will enable you greet the people, problems and events that you encounter throughout your day optimistically and cheerfully. Your attitude will determine how well you solve problems. When you hit a wall in your bid to provide solutions, your attitude will determine if you will keep going until you break through that wall. Your attitude speaks volumes. It can be the difference between you getting a 'no vacancy' or 'you're urgently needed' decision from an employer/customer. As a problem solver, your attitude counts.

TAKE CHARGE OF YOUR ATTITUDE

One morning I went to a bank to carry out a transaction. There was limited parking space so I had to wait a while in my car for a space to become vacant. By the time a space became available for me, I was already running out of patience. I was directed to a parking spot by a guard from the bank. After parking, I got out of my car and began to walk towards the bank's entrance, only to realize I had left my phone in the car.

Biting back my frustration, I hurried back to my car. As I was fumbling for my keys a different guard appeared, asking me to re-park my car. I looked around for the guard who had directed me to park at that spot but couldn't find him. I tried to explain to the new guard that his colleague had supervised my parking and so this was no fault of mine; his colleague was to blame. The guard refused to budge. No matter what I said he just kept saying, "Sir, you have to re-park."

At this point I had lost all patience. I had hoped to get in and out of the bank in a jiffy; yet, after having spent several minutes just waiting to park my car, this guard stood prepared to waste even more of my time insisting I fix a mistake that was not my fault in the first place. I did not bother trying to hide how upset I was. But after all was said and done I had to re-park. All this while, the security man had kept a calm demeanour.

I got into the banking hall, completed my transaction and walked back to my car. As soon as I turned on the ignition the same guard stepped up to help guide me out. When I was finally positioned to drive off, he leaned toward my car window and, with a sincere smile, said, "Have a nice day, sir." As I drove away, I thought to myself, that's a great attitude. I would never have expected the guard to show such a positive attitude so soon after that incident. In my experience, most employees would hardly spare a glance at me after that, but this man chose to be positive all the way.

Your attitude is an indicator of the person you really are inside. We often blame our negative behaviour on circumstances or on other people, like we have no real choice or control over our reactions. Many employees claim that their unprofessional or downright rude behaviour is often as a result of their treatment at the hands of a customer, colleague or employer. But whenever you point a finger at someone else, you should be aware that three other fingers point back at you. This might be unpleasant to hear, but the truth is that *you* alone are responsible for programming your attitude.

You have to take responsibility for your behaviour. Every day you choose your attitude toward people, situations, ideas and life; only you can choose to exhibit the right attitude. If by choosing negative feelings, beliefs and actions you exhibit a negative attitude, nobody can change it. Negativity is toxic, and your negative attitude will only serve to drive people away from you. Choosing the right attitude is your responsibility. Your attitude is under the direct control of your will. You can decide what it is going to be every moment of the day, and every day of your life.

CHOOSE TO FEEL GREAT EVERY DAY

At the New Covenant Baptist Church, Chicago, Illinois, on 9 April 1967, Martin Luther King Jr. said, "If a man is called to be a street sweeper, he should sweep streets even as a Michelangelo painted, as Handel and Beethoven composed music or Shakespeare wrote poetry. He should sweep streets so well that all the hosts of heaven and earth will pause to say, 'Here lived a great street sweeper who did his job well.'" Most people would see sweeping as a menial and boring job.

77

However, the issue is not with the assignment but with how you choose to feel as you execute it. This is important because how you feel determines how well you will carry out the assignment.

How well you choose to carry out a given assignment is what will cause you to stand out. 'How well' is not just about your technical ability; it includes your disposition. A certain traffic warden in our city always dances as he directs traffic. I find it remarkable that with all the negative experiences at home, at work, and in our country in general, this man chooses every day to keep his dance. I see many traffic wardens each day, but with this man his choice to keep his dance stands him out. He chooses every day to feel great no matter what.

Each morning you wake up you have two choices. You can choose to be in a great mood or you can choose to be in a bad mood. Each time something unpleasant happens to you, you can choose to be a victim or you can choose to learn from it and move on. Every time someone comes to you complaining, you can choose to accept their complaining or you can point out the positive side of life.

No matter what happens, you can choose to feel great. Feeling great often causes you to experience the great results you desire. The great results will then reinforce your choice to feel great.

ACT WITH CONFIDENCE

With confidence, you win even before you begin. Here is a story that illustrates this:

The business executive was deep in debt and could see no way out; creditors were closing in on him. He sat on the park bench, head in hands, wondering if anything could save his company from bankruptcy. Suddenly an old man

appeared before him. "I can see that something is troubling you," he said. After listening to the executive's woes, the old man said, "I believe I can help you." He asked the man his name and wrote out a check. He pushed it into his hand, and said, "Take this money. Meet me here exactly one year from today, and you can pay me back at that time." Then he turned and disappeared as quickly as he had come.

The business executive saw in his hand a check for $500,000, signed by John D. Rockefeller, then one of the richest men in the world! "I can erase my money worries in an instant!" he thought. But instead, he decided to put the uncashed check in his safe. Just knowing it was there might give him the strength to work out a way to save his business.

With renewed optimism, he negotiated better deals and extended terms of payment. He closed several big sales. Within a few months, he was out of debt and making money once again. Exactly one year later, he returned to the park with the uncashed check. At the agreed-upon time, the old man appeared. But just as the executive was about to hand back the check and share his success story, a nurse came running up and grabbed the old man. "I'm so glad I caught him!" she cried. "I hope he hasn't been bothering you. He's always escaping from the rest home and telling people he's John D. Rockefeller." And she led the old man away by the arm.

The astonished executive just stood there, stunned. All year long he'd been wheeling and dealing, buying and selling, convinced he had half a million dollars behind him. Suddenly, he realized that it wasn't the money, real or imagined, that had turned his life around. It was his newfound self-confidence that gave him the power to achieve anything he went after.[3]

The business executive had won before he started again because of his renewed confidence.

To show confidence you need to be able to assert yourself. Being assertive means having the ability to express your thoughts and feelings in a way that clearly states your needs. It does not mean being aggressive; it means being firm. Assertiveness results in being heard, included and recognized, and this boosts your confidence.

You are gifted at something, and you can attain any objective you set out to achieve. If you can lay aside your fear of failing and focus all your attention on attaining your goal, you will act with more confidence; and with confidence in yourself you can generate the enthusiasm required to reflect a positive image of your problem solving ability to employers and customers.

If I asked you these questions, what would your answers be: Who are you? Why are you here? What makes you significant? What is your true value? Where are you going? What do you want to achieve? What price do you have to pay to achieve your goal? Are you daily paying this price? When you know the answers to these questions your confidence soars. If you have no answers, then your attitude will show no confidence. It is simple: you cannot confidently sell something if you do not know and understand its purpose - the solution it provides. You cannot sell yourself confidently if you do not know, understand and see yourself as a solution.

All your learning, training and self-development should be aimed at one thing —making you feel more confident about your ability to provide solutions. The more knowledge you have of how to produce a desired result, the more confident you become. Confidence comes when we know who we are, what makes us significant. It comes when you know you have value to offer.

SHOW YOUR PASSION

Imagine this scenario: a young man says to his girlfriend, "You are a nice girl and I'm really interested in you. Will you marry me?" Another young man says to his girlfriend, "I think about you all day, and I see you in my dreams. My heart skips when I see you, and I feel restless when I can't get to you. I want to spend the rest of my life with you. I love you. Will you marry me?" Who do you think will most likely get the desired result? The second man, of course, because every woman wants her man to be passionate about her.

Most people complain about the problems around them, but ask them for a solution and they will say 'it's not my problem.' You will find many people who start out saying how badly they need a job. Then they get employed and they hate the job, hate their employers and hate the problems that customers daily present them with. Of course, such people are the first to be relieved of their jobs during a downsizing or retrenchment exercise. Similarly, jobseekers often wonder why they do not get employed after an interview process. They may have the right academic qualifications but they often lack one of the vital ingredients that employers look for —passion.

People love to associate and work with passionate people. When you are passionate about solving problems you easily stand out from the crowd. Passion can be felt because it is contagious. Once I was to fly from Abuja to Port Harcourt and had to stand in line to be checked in. As I got closer to the front desk I noticed something: of the two staff members of the airline company attending to passengers, one looked bored, like he was just going through a routine and would rather not be there. The other wore a smile that made you believe he was excited to serve you, and he worked fast to ensure that people got through quickly. I happened to be on the queue for the enthusiastic staff member. When it got to my turn I smiled and said, "I like the way you do your job." He replied, "Thank you." He took my computer printout, looked at it, and said with a smile, "Where would you like to sit?" He was passionate about serving his customer.

Organizations are built and sustained by passionate people. For this reason employers seek people that are passionate about what their company does, or rather, the problems their company solves to make a profit. Customers seek solutions from people that are passionate about what they do. They know that passionate people make the necessary investment to be the best at what they do. This ensures they always provide the best solutions.

Daily we meet people who just go through the motions at their jobs. They can't wait for Fridays. The alarm on Monday mornings is a wake-up call to their worst nightmare. Passionate people produce outstanding results because of the drive they have for what they do. They love what they do and it shows in the enthusiasm with which they do it.

Passion is a quality that problem solvers have. You can only

82

provide a desirable solution if you are passionate about solving the problem. You have to focus on solving problems you are passionate about so you can be and give your best.

BE POSITIVE

Do roses have thorns or do thorns have roses? It all boils down to how you think about it. Do you see the rose or the thorn? Do you see an overwhelming problem or a great opportunity? Do you focus on the problem or do you focus on solutions? Do your thoughts move toward the negative or toward the positive?

Focusing your thoughts on the negative is like tripping yourself up. The outcome is a downward spiral to failure before you even begin. Here is a story that illustrates the outcome of focusing on the negative:

> McGinty, a farmer, needed to plough his field before the dry spell set in, but his own plough had broken.
>
> "I know, I'll ask my neighbour, farmer Murphy, to borrow his plough. He's a good man; I'm sure he'll have done his ploughing by now and he'll be glad to lend me his machine."
>
> So McGinty began to walk the three or four fields to Murphy's farm.
>
> After a field of walking, McGinty says to himself, "I hope that Murphy has finished all his own ploughing or he'll not be able to lend me his machine..."
>
> Then after a few more minutes of worrying and walking,

McGinty says to himself, "And what if Murphy's plough is old and on its last legs — he'll never be wanting to lend it to me will he (sic)?"

And after another field, McGinty says, "Murphy was never a very helpful fellow. I reckon maybe he won't be too keen to lend me his plough even if it's in perfect working order and he's finished all his own ploughing weeks ago...."

As McGinty arrives at Murphy's farm, McGinty is thinking, "That old Murphy can be a mean old fellow. I reckon even if he's got all his ploughing done, and his own machine is sitting there doing nothing, he'll not lend it to me just so he can watch me go to ruin..."

McGinty walks up Murphy's front path, knocks on the door, and Murphy answers.

"Well good morning Mr McGinty, what can I do for you?" says Murphy.

And McGinty says, with eyes bulging, "You can take your bloody plough, and you can stick it up your bloody arse!"[4]

McGinty had engaged in so much negative thinking that he did not even try asking Murphy for the plough and waiting to hear his reply. He concluded, through his negative internal monologue, that Murphy had already said no. He became indignant for no reason and insulted poor Murphy. People who always have problems with their employers and customers always think about them from a negative perspective. If you could read such people's thoughts you would hear things like 'my boss is such a pain in the neck', 'here comes another headache; I hate these whiny customers,' 'I hate this job'.

In the Bible Apostle Paul recommends: "Finally, my brothers, whatever is true, whatever is honourable, whatever is just, whatever is pure, whatever is lovely, whatever is commendable, if anything is worthy of praise, think about these things." By dwelling on negative thoughts you are setting yourself up for failure. Negative thinking and providing solutions do not go together; combining them will be like trying to sell a product you already believe people won't buy. Your effort to sell will be half-hearted. You will be rude and dismissive with potential customers, because you do not expect them to buy anyway. Like McGinty, you will see negative outcomes before you even truly attempt to solve the problem.

On the other hand, when you focus on positive thoughts you will take actions that are congruent with this thought pattern and produce the desired positive outcome. If you always see opportunity in the midst of difficulty you will focus on solutions rather than the difficulty.

You need to have a positive outlook regardless of your circumstances, because there will always be thorns around the roses you desire. There will be times when you put in your best yet don't get the results you want immediately. Thomas Edison tried 999 times to perfect the light bulb but did not succeed until the 1,000th time. The way he saw it, the 999 'failed' attempts weren't really failures; they just meant he had discovered 999 ways *not* to invent the light bulb. He had a positive outlook. He saw the undesirable outcomes as part of the process to achieving his goal. Don't let any setback get you to stop. Shake it off and keep moving. Maintaining a positive mindset helps you focus on positive actions that you can take toward achieving your goal.

To maintain a positive mindset you have to control your thoughts. Research shows that a human being has about 12,000 to 60,000 thoughts a day. There are lots of events in life that can cause your thoughts to spiral toward the negative. Imagine if all the 60,000 thoughts you have in a day are negative. All the actions that will follow from those thoughts will lead you to a day of complete despair. But imagine if all your thoughts are positive. Your actions will lead you to overcome challenges and solve problems in a proactive manner.

If you find yourself entertaining negative thoughts, you can stop them by consciously and deliberately focusing on positive ones. A few simple ways to change the flow of your thoughts are by reading a book, talking to positive people, reading and recalling quotes that motivate you, or listening to inspiring audio programs. Filling your mind with positive information and being around positive people will change the way you see things. You will start to view life from a positive angle and, before long, your attitude and actions will follow suit.

BE COMMITTED

A person who is committed will give everything in support of an undertaking or a cause they believe in without turning back or giving up. Here is a story that vividly makes this point:

> The Olympic Games, Mexico, 1968. The marathon is the final event on the program. The Olympic stadium is packed and there is excitement as the first athlete, an Ethiopian runner, enters the stadium. The crowd erupts as he crosses the finish line.

Way back in the field is another runner, John Stephen Akwhari of Tanzania. He has been eclipsed by the other runners. After 30 kilometres his head is throbbing, his muscles are aching and he falls to the ground. He has serious leg injuries and officials want him to retire, but he refuses. With his knee bandaged Akwhari picks himself up and hobbles the remaining 12 kilometres to the finish line. An hour after the winner has finished Akwhari enters the stadium. All but a few thousand of the crowd has gone home. Akwhari moves around the track at a painstakingly slow pace, until finally he collapses over the finish line.

It is one of the most heroic efforts of Olympic history. Afterward, asked by a reporter why he had not dropped out, Akwhari says, "My country did not send me to start the race. They sent me to finish."[5]

Commitment means finishing the course no matter what. According to the Bible, when Jesus Christ died on the cross the gospels record that he said, "It is finished." He was committed to his purpose of saving mankind, even though it meant dying. Nelson Mandela spent years in prison for his stance against apartheid. In the Rivonia treason trial of 1964, facing his sentence, Mandela made this statement in court:

I have fought against white domination, and I have fought against black domination. I have cherished the ideal of a democratic and free society in which all persons live together in harmony and with equal

87

opportunities. It is an ideal which I hope to live for and to achieve. But if needs be, it is an ideal for which I am prepared to die.

To be committed means you either win or die fighting. It means burning all bridges that lead back to your comfort zones. Stories have been told of how generals have burnt bridges behind their troops to make retreat impossible and, thus, forced their soldiers to be totally committed and to fight for their lives. When there is only one option, people commit. Give yourself only one option —becoming a highly sought after problem solver.

Unless commitment is made there are only 'plans to do' but no actions taken. Commitment leads to continuous persistent action, and continuous persistent action leads to solving problems, and being rewarded for it.

You need to commit. Don't just be involved. Set yourself apart by choosing to be committed to providing solutions for your employers/customers. Do not offer half-hearted service. Choose to do a great job. Be self-motivated. Do not depend on others to spark your drive to achieve, but choose to be courageous and to commit.

BE GRATEFUL

Everyone feels down from time to time. Sometimes everything seems to be working against you, and you feel like lashing out or screaming at someone, or even throwing in the towel and walking away. At such times the last thing you feel like doing is giving your best.

When you feel like the world has conspired against you, know that you still have a choice —the choice to either be part of the problem or a solution to the problem. You can simply stop and start to count your blessings. Regardless of your present circumstance, if you are candid with yourself you will find that there is something to be grateful for. Focus on the things that you can be thankful for, and you will suddenly find your disposition becoming positive.

Gratitude leads to a positive attitude. If you are grateful for the job you have you will find that you will be positive toward your employer/customer. When you are grateful for all the good you have enjoyed you will feel more positive about your future. This feeling raises your energy level and causes you to take action geared toward getting desirable results. Keeping an attitude of gratitude helps you overcome your challenges. Only positive people can be grateful, so adopting an attitude of gratitude at all times immediately places you in a positive state of mind.

This might sound impossible, but you should also be grateful for whatever problems you may be facing. If you never had problems how would you know you could solve them? No one can build great triceps and biceps without going through some pain at the gym. In the same way, no one can build problem solving muscles without experiencing and solving problems. Facing and solving problems is a necessity if you must climb the ladder of success in life. The hard knocks you get are part of your training. Choosing gratitude changes your perspective and puts you in the right frame of mind to handle challenges, solve problems and obtain the rewards you desire.

LET IT GO

A person's inability to let go of a perceived offence from an employer or customer can greatly affect the attitude with which they solve problems. If for any reason you choose not to forgive someone, know that you will be sabotaging yourself. If you do not forgive you will tend to harbour bitterness that will affect your productivity. Nobody can be their best when they are bitter or angry.

Lewis B. Smedes said, "To forgive is to set a prisoner free and discover that the prisoner was you." When you work a job while feeling bitter or resentful toward your employer or customer, you imprison the best of you. You will never give your best to solving problems in this state. On the other hand, when you forgive an offence you become at peace with yourself. When a person is at peace their level of productivity is high because their mind is free from any sort of clutter.

Just like you, other humans have flaws. Being forgiving enables you to accept other people's flaws. It helps you realize that sometimes your expectations of others might be unrealistic, and you just have to deal with it. Reframing a negative statement or behaviour in a positive way helps you to let it go. Your ability to let go ensures that your attitude remains positive regardless of negative statements or behaviour from your employers/customers. A negative attitude cannot drive out a negative attitude; only a positive attitude can.

Imagine this scenario: a customer walks into the business premises of a company and gives vent to her anger over an unresolved issue, and the company's officer snaps back at her. What do you think would be the outcome of this? A prolonged exchange of more negative statements, anger and insults —and, of course, an unresolved problem and possibly a lost customer.

If on the other hand the company's officer listens to the enraged customer, overlooking her delivery and focusing on the problem, his or her attitude will be positive toward the customer. The officer may not like the customer's approach, but that is beyond his or her control. What the officer can control is his or her own attitude and desire to provide a solution. Solving the problem will affect the customer's attitude and might even result in an apology from said customer.

Choose to be responsive rather than reactive. Choose to let it go. Oftentimes, the people toward whom you harbour unforgiveness are unaware of your feelings, and so they carry on unaffected while you sabotage yourself by carrying a negative attitude. Being unforgiving is very costly; it affects your inner peace and productivity and, worse still, you bear the cost alone.

You have a duty to yourself to protect your inner economy (your heart) from being eroded by bitterness and hatred that will hinder your progress. If your inner economy is destroyed you will not be your best at solving problems for employers/customers. You should choose to forgive no matter what. It profits you more.

THIS IS COMMON SENSE

1. You attitude is critical to your success as a problem solver.

2. Your attitude defines how you see and act toward a situation, person or idea.

3. Your attitude is made up of three components: what you feel, what you think or believe and how you behave.

4. You can control your attitude by the choices you make in the areas of these three components.

5. You are the only person responsible for your attitude, and you can improve it instantaneously.

6. If you choose to intentionally solve problems with a great

91

attitude every day your results and rewards will greatly multiply.

ACTION EXERCISES

1. What is your attitude when you encounter problems or when things go wrong?

2. Write down the negative attitudes you often find yourself engaging in.

3. Write down positive attitudes that you can choose to display in the various situations you have noted for action exercise 2, and then take action to implement an attitude change immediately.

Note

[3] http://www.enmore.org/stories-main-page.htm

[4] http://www.businessballs.com/stories.htm#the-gardener%27s-badge-story

[5] http://storiesforpreaching.com/category/sermonillustrations/commitment/

Chapter Seven

CONNECT

….the wise build bridges and the foolish build dams.

- Nigerian proverb

Your success as a problem solver is greatly dependent on your ability to communicate the value you bring. You can have brilliant solutions, but if you can't get them across they won't get you anywhere. You may be the person with the required skills for the job, but if you can't communicate this you won't get the job. If you are unable to communicate your solution effectively you will fail at the point of selling yourself, your product, service or idea. And if your solution is not sold you won't get the reward you desire. This means we have to learn how to communicate effectively.

Most people make the mistake of giving information and thinking they have communicated. A big problem in communication is the illusion that it has taken place when words are spoken. Have you ever given someone an instruction and then they did something else, and when you asked them why they did that they simply replied, 'That's what I thought you told me to do'? Or have you ever performed a task only to be told that what you did was not what you had been instructed to do? If you have you will agree that giving or getting information is not the same thing as communicating.

Informing is giving out, but communicating is getting through. Your being able to inform an employer or customer about yourself, your service or a situation does not necessarily translate into communication. You need to get through. You need to connect.

Whatever you are trying to achieve, connecting with the people concerned will help you. But if you are unable to connect, it will cost you. The cost may be the loss of a job, loss of a promotion, loss of more earnings, loss of a potential customer, loss of the sale of your idea or loss of a major deal you are brokering.

What we mean by 'connect' is being able to identify and relate to people in a way that makes them comfortable with you, trust you and feel that you share their concern; and as a result of this you increase your influence with them. Have you ever met someone for the first time and after talking to them you felt like you had known them your whole life, or that they were somebody you had been looking for? This is as a result of a connection between you and the person. Everybody talks but not everyone connects.

CONNECT INTENTIONALLY

From the moment anyone first meets us, they are consciously or unconsciously evaluating us. Once we begin speaking they start to decide if they should keep listening to us or dismiss us. People make quick judgments about us, and so we have to be intentional when we communicate, to ensure that we connect and get our message across.

To communicate and connect intentionally, you need to be committed to intentional living. People need to feel your commitment to the solution you are offering. You need to show that you are all in; committed to going the extra mile to deliver solutions that will meet and even exceed expectations.

We once conducted a sales training for the staff of a particular organization. During the training, there was a practical session where the staff members were to make presentations meant for prospective customers using some of the techniques they had just learned. It was a role playing scenario showing possible objections prospective customers could raise during a sales call and ways to handle these objections. After the session everyone could see why certain staff members were bringing in little or no business. Despite the fact that they had been given a week to prepare, their communication lacked effort and commitment. The result was lost deals again and again. The staff members in question made no effort to intentionally connect with their prospective customers. Sadly, a few months later some of them were fired for non-performance. The leader of the company felt they had been given enough opportunity to improve and prove themselves. Anyone that lives intentionally will not allow such a thing to happen to them. We know you won't let such happen to you, so commit to intentionally connect when you communicate.

PREPARE TO CONNECT

Segun is a well-respected chief executive in the Nigerian business environment. He always goes into a negotiation to win —failure is not an option for him. However, his success does not happen by sheer luck or some form of magic. He has a simple formula —know everything about everything concerning the deal to be negotiated, especially from the customer's perspective.

To him, preparation meant success. If he was able to connect with the customer he knew he had a high probability of winning the deal. He would research the customer from both a professional and a personal angle. He would ask himself questions like:

What are the customer's objectives?

What would the customer consider a win?

What are the customer's personal lifestyle choices and preferences?

If I were the customer talking to me, what would I want to know?

If I were in the customer's position, what would I ask me?

He believes that his ability to answer these questions correctly increases his chances of winning the deal. The focus of Segun's preparation is to always leave an impression in the mind of the customer that will get his company the deal. He finds it quite amazing that as commonsensical and easy as this principle is, many of his competitors do not seem to practise it.

Intentional communication produces results for those who work at it. If you think that just because you have no problem talking to others on any subject that comes to mind you connect when you communicate, you are getting it all wrong. Being able to talk is not the same thing as getting through. To intentionally connect you have to prepare. You need to get insight that will enable you connect. Before you meet new people, before you make that very important call, do your homework. Determine where the other party's needs and interests lie. Make that connection between them and you.

You need to be clear when you communicate the solution you are offering to an employer/customer. You have to be particularly clear about two things: first, about your skills and abilities —and you will need to demonstrate confidence in yourself to do this. Be clear about what you can and can't do. Second, you need to be clear about the employer's/customer's goal. Who are they? What are their interests? Why would they need you or your product? What are their expectations? What do you have to offer them? What do you want them to know? How do you want them to feel after meeting with you? What do you want them to do after you leave? Ask yourself: *'If I were in their position, what would I ask me?'* Being clear about these questions will enable you prepare to communicate and connect. Outline the key points you want to make about yourself. Think of possible hard questions and how you will answer them. Write them down if possible. The whole idea is that you must prepare. Don't wing it. Prepare!

MAKE IT MORE ABOUT THEM THAN ABOUT YOU —ASK QUESTIONS

Employers respect people who display the initiative to ask intelligent questions about their company. It shows that you are prepared, and that you care —two very persuasive qualities. You learn about your employer/customer by asking questions. But it is amazing to note how little effort people make to ask potential employers/customers about themselves.

During interview sessions we sometimes meet people who made no attempt whatsoever to learn about the company they had applied to. When you do not ask questions about your prospective employer/customer, it simply shows that you are not really interested in them. It shows that they don't matter to you, and you don't care about them or their problems. To them, all you care about is what you can get from them for yourself. If they get this impression of you, you have already lost the job. *Sorry, no vacancy*!

At the close of an interview candidates are often asked, 'Do you have any questions?' The answer most candidates give is 'no', effectively throwing away this opportunity to 'close the deal.' When you are given the opportunity to ask questions it is your chance to take charge of the conversation and make your final attempts to sell yourself. Asking questions shows you are prepared, and that you care enough to want to find out how you can do a great job for your employer or customer. The people who connect with employers or customers are those who are best at getting what they want by asking intelligent questions, thereby uncovering real needs and concerns. They ask questions to expand the conversation and to increase their understanding of the important issues, and then they can adapt their approach to foster connection. By asking the right questions you can demonstrate your understanding of relevant problems, and show how you can implement possible solutions using your knowledge, skill and expertise.

MAKE IT MORE ABOUT THEM THAN ABOUT YOU —LISTEN

Communicating effectively starts with listening. As problem solvers, if we want to connect when we communicate, we need to listen twice as much as we speak. Our primary focus as humans is ourselves and our interests, and so we tend to talk more about what we want. The fact, however, is that to get what we want, we need to focus more on knowing and talking about what employers/customers want. To know what they want, you need to listen to their concerns. If they get what they want you will be in a better position to negotiate and get what *you* want.

Listening can be difficult because it requires giving up our focus on ourselves and on our interests. During the course of training for a particular company, the managing director asked us to attend certain meetings and observe, to see how we could help the staff members improve on their jobs. The few times we were invited to such meetings, we noticed that the managing director kept saying the same thing to one member of staff: "You don't listen." That staff member would talk and talk to justify her actions, without ever listening to understand. She made no attempt to learn the skill of listening. In the end, due to her habit of not listening she took actions that caused her to lose her job.

In Shakespeare's *Julius Caesar*, Marc Anthony admonishes the Romans, "Be silent that you may hear." Your listening ability greatly impacts your ability to connect. When we listen we learn and understand. If we don't listen we cannot learn and get understanding; and the extent to which we understand employers/customers is the extent to which we can effectively communicate the solutions we have to offer.

Here is a list of benefits that the skill of listening offers:

- You will learn from what you hear.

- You will show the people to whom you listen that you're interested in them.

- You will gain insight into the ways others perceive their individual needs, desires and motivations.

- You will give others a chance to let down their guard so that they can hear what you have to say.

- You will actively involve others in the communication process.

- You will clarify misconceptions.

When you listen, remember to also listen with your eyes. The most important thing in communication is to hear what isn't being said. Research shows that in communication words account for seven percent of the message, tone of voice for 38 percent and body language for 55 percent. The things that aren't being said with words account for a very high percentage of the message. So you have to look for feelings. Watch out for facial expressions and other nonverbal signals. Attending seminars and reading books on communication can go a long way in helping you understand the nonverbal aspects of communication and help you listen better.

Here is a story that clearly illustrates the importance of listening.

Many years ago, a young man went to a Western Union office to apply for a job as a telegrapher. In those days, messages were still transmitted in Morse code through audible clicks.

The young man had no experience in telegraphy, but he had studied it at home and knew the code.

His heart sank as he walked into the office and looked over the crowd of people filling out application forms.

As he sat down with his own form, he heard a clicking noise in the background. He stopped filling out his form and listened. Then he dashed into the nearby office. Moments later, a man emerged and told the other applicants they could go home. The job had just been filled.

What got him the job?

The clicking noise was the sound of a telegraph receiver. The young man listened and translated the clicks into words: "If you understand this message, come into the office. The job is yours."[6]

The young man listened, connected and got the job. Listening pays in the marketplace. When employers interview candidates for positions they spend about 70 to 90 percent of their time listening. Great salespeople listen to customers to find out what their needs are, and then they concentrate on meeting those needs. The best of negotiators know that no progress can be made until they have heard and understood what the other party wants. If you first listen and understand the needs of an employer/customer, you will have armed yourself to effectively communicate to connect.

COMMUNICATE THE RIGHT ATTITUDE

People may hear our words, but they feel our attitude. That will either enable us to connect with them and win them over, or it will alienate them and cause us to lose them. Our attitude, which is nonverbal, often overpowers the words we use when we communicate to others.

The feeling you communicate when you are with employers/customers matters a lot. Are you communicating 'I'm so enthused to work with you', or are you communicating 'let's just get it over with; I'd rather not be here'? In his book, *How to Talk to Anyone, Anytime, Anywhere,* CNN's Larry King shares how he got his first job in broadcasting because of his enthusiasm, even though he had no experience. His advice is this: "Communicate your enthusiasm for the job." You need to convey a sense of energy and enthusiasm that says 'I'm ready to go; I'm ready to start right now.'

People want to be sure they can trust you, and so another very important message your attitude should communicate to employers/customers is 'I'm here to serve your concerns', 'I'm here to help you achieve your goal', 'You can trust me to give you the best solution.' Mind you, this can't be faked. This attitude will show if you really care about your employer/customer.

We were once invited to conduct interview sessions for a company alongside another Human Resource consultant. In the course of the interview one candidate caught our interest. He was well-groomed, charming and well-spoken. He seemed suited for the position he had applied for, but just to be sure about him we asked more questions. After we were done he stepped out and the HR consultant simply said, "He is good but his only interest is in how much he will gain through the use of the resources of the company. He is not here to work." With what we had seen and heard, we concurred. All his smart talk couldn't cover the fact that he did not really care about the needs of the employer. He saw his employer as a ladder to be used and discarded. His attitude spoke and gave him away.

MAKE THEM LISTEN TO YOU —FOCUS ON THEIR AGENDA

At an international meeting of company executives, one American business-person asked an executive from Japan what he regarded as the most important language for world trade. The American thought the answer would be English. But the executive from Japan, who had a more holistic understanding of business, smiled and replied, "My customer's language."[7]

If you want to connect, speak the language of employers/customers. Focus on their agenda. Abraham Lincoln said, "When I'm getting ready to reason with a man, I spend one-third of my time thinking about myself and what I am going to say —and two-thirds thinking about him and what he is going to say." This statement is insightful because it shows us what we should give more thought to when communicating to connect —the interests of employers/customers. You get people to do the things you require them to do by presenting your arguments in terms of their interests, in terms of what they want to be, have or do.

To effectively connect you have to look at what your employer/customer wants. You have to get on their agenda and try to see things from their point of view. Think from their perspective and concentrate on what would be important to them. Sonya Hamlin in her book, *How to Talk so People Listen*, explains: "To make anyone listen while you try to get your message across, you must always answer the listener's instinctive question: 'Why should I listen to you? What's in it for me if I let you in?'" You need to make their concern your concern, and position yourself as the solution to their concern.

To position yourself as the solution to their concern you need to communicate what you know, what you can do and how it will serve their interests. Stating one of the cardinal rules for selling yourself, Larry King advises: "Show prospective employers what you can do for them. What do you bring that is unique? ...Ask not what your employer can do for you but what you can do for your employer... Don't tell your interviewer what's on your resume which they've already read. Tell them how you can do this job better than anybody else would."

Sell the advantages you bring. Sell the benefits you are offering and not your features. A feature is a fact or quality about you, your

103

product or idea. The benefit is how this fact or quality will help your employer/customer achieve their goal or solve their problem. Do this by showing how your knowledge, skills, expertise or contacts will be used to solve their problems. You have to find out their primary agenda and offer solutions to their issues. Possible employer/customer concerns include:

- Increasing revenue

- Reducing costs

- Becoming more profitable

- Improving efficiency

- Improving quality

- Improving customer service

- Gaining more influence in the marketplace

- Developing new and better products or systems

- Innovative idea generation

- Increasing brand recognition in the marketplace

- Increasing product or service sales

- Increasing cash flow

If your employer/customer finds that personal connection between your message and their own objective, you are on your way to getting the job, getting the promotion, closing the deal, selling the product or getting whatever might be your desired reward. Shared concern creates connection. If their concerns become your concern, when you communicate you will connect.

BE THE KIND OF PERSON
PEOPLE WANT TO CONNECT WITH

My co-author is the kind of person people would want to connect with. From my experiences with him I can confidently say he is a man that practices the core principle of connecting —focusing on others. In spite of his tight schedule he makes out time to help others. He does this not because it is convenient but because this is who he is.

Speaking about Jesus Christ in the Bible, Apostle Paul said, "For we do not have a High Priest who is unable to understand and sympathize and have a shared feeling with our weaknesses and infirmities…" The gospels show that Jesus shared the concerns of people. He touched their pain points and provided the help they desperately needed. This is why people connected with him. If you want employers/customers to connect with you, you need to touch their pain points. You need to be the kind of person who will understand and share their concerns, as well as offer appropriate solutions to help them. This is how you become the kind of person people would want to connect with. Seek first to genuinely help employers and customers; find out who they are and what is important to them. This makes connecting more natural and less forced.

THIS IS COMMON SENSE

1. Your ability to effectively communicate your solutions to employers and customers is the key to getting the rewards you desire.

2. Communication is about getting through.

3. Getting through is about connecting with others.

4. You need to connect intentionally. Plan and prepare to connect.

5. You connect by focusing on the interests and agenda of employers and customers.

6. If you make a habit of helping employers/customers with their concerns, they will definitely want to connect with you; and this means you get your reward.

ACTION EXERCISES

1. Write out some of the common concerns of employers and customers.

2. Write out your plan to communicate you solutions, and prepare a presentation.

3. Practice your presentation, highlighting the pain points or interests of your employer/customer and showing how you would solve their problems with your knowledge, skill and expertise

Notes

[6]Nido R. Qubein, *How to Be a Great Communicator: In Person, on Paper, and on the Podium* (New York: John Wiley) 1996

[7]John C. Maxwell, *Everyone Communicates, Few Connect* (Thomas Nelson) 2010

Chapter Eight

UNDERSTANDING THE VALUE CHAIN

A family is like a forest; it looks dense from the outside,

but when you are inside you see that each tree has its place.

- African proverb

For every organization there is a value chain, and the individuals who work in the organization must fit somewhere along this value chain. First, let us define a value chain and why it is important. Thereafter, we shall discuss the individual's place on the value chain, why it is important to locate your place on the value chain and, more importantly, why it is crucial to move up the value chain and how. Finally, we shall discuss how money follows you up the value chain.

A loose definition offered in Wikipedia states that "A *value chain* is a chain of activities that a firm operating in a specific industry performs in order to deliver a valuable product or service for the market." More clearly, Investopedia informs: "Value-chain analysis looks at every step a business goes through, from raw materials to the eventual end-user. The goal is to deliver maximum value for the least possible total cost." *The Economic Times* defined and described value chain in these terms:

> A value chain is the whole series of activities
> that create and build value at every step. The
> total value delivered by the company is the sum
> total of the value built up all throughout the

company. Michael Porter developed this concept in his 1980 book, *Competitive Advantage*. In describing the significance of the value chain he states, "The value chain concept separates useful activities (which allow the company as a whole to gain competitive advantage) from the wasteful activities (which hinder the company from getting a lead in the market). Focusing on the value-creating activities could give the company many advantages. For example, the ability to charge higher prices; lower cost of manufacture; better brand image, faster response to threats or opportunities."

IT'S ALL ABOUT ADDING VALUE

From the various definitions, we see that every organization exists to provide some form of added value in order to get paid. No organization gets or appropriates value if their system is not set up to add value. Value addition can apply to goods or services. From the definition by *The Economic Times*, it is clear that along the chain, value is expected to be added. This is because the total value derived at the end by the organization is the sum total of all the value added along the chain. Note also that for most organizations, wasteful activities within their establishment are a huge source of concern, one that management is often willing to have significantly reduced or totally eliminated.

In order to explain the value chain concept properly, let us take a look at a simple dry cleaner's value chain:

1. Picking up customers' dirty clothing (for those who provide

pick up service)

2. Sorting the clothes and tagging them appropriately for washing and also for reference

3. Purchase of dry-cleaning consumable materials (washing liquid, detergent, softener etc.)

4. Actual cleaning and washing

5. Ironing, sorting and packaging for collection/delivery

6. Collection outlet and customer management centre

7. Payment, collection and accounting

8. Delivery of cleaned clothes and fabric (for those who provide such value added service)

9. Management of staff (human resources)

10. Logistics and office administration

11. Information technology and management

12. General management

As can be seen from the activities of the simple dry cleaning office, Activities 1 to 7 are referred to in Michael Porter's book as the *Primary Activities* while Activities 8 to 12 are referred to as *Support Activities*. On each of the lines/chains of activities, value is expected to be added in order to be able to charge the customer for work done. The difference between how much it costs the firm to provide the final output and the amount the customer pays is called the margin. In other words, every activity on the chain must seek to reduce the cost to the company and increase the margin for the company.

CLARIFY YOUR POSITION ON THE VALUE CHAIN

The concept of value chain is extremely important to any organization because it helps the organization break down the entire business into clear points of value addition. It also throws light on what activities the management of an organization considers wasteful or useful, and points out the wasteful activities they might be engaging in —whether ignorantly or by choice. It helps the management to see which activities require particular attention in terms of human and capital resources. This concept provides monitoring and visible intervention points for management and workers. For decision makers, it helps in reorganization or outright elimination of a set of activities along the value chain if those activities are not generating the desired outcome, or if they are eroding rather than adding value to the organization.

It is critical that as an employee or entrepreneur, you identify your place on the value chain. You need to understand the relative importance of the activity you perform on the value chain, and the relative importance of your position within the value chain. This analysis is important for the following reasons:

1. It helps you to assess your relative importance within the organisation and your relative level of indispensability.

2. It helps you to categorise your activities as either wasteful or useful.

3. It helps you to locate your role as either *Primary* or *Support*.

4. It helps you to see the bigger picture and chart a course for growth.

5. It helps you to plan and optimise your potential within an organisation.

In the case of a would-be employee:

1. It helps you to understand the company and what is important to it.

2. It helps you to research for positioning within the organization.

3. It helps position you where you will ultimately grow and be of service to the company.

4. It helps you to understand if the company can provide the growth requirement for your career.

5. It helps you to know if you can provide value to the organization given your knowledge and skill set.

6. It helps you to decide if the company is a good fit for you.

CLARIFY HOW TO MOVE UP THE CHAIN

Organizations hire primarily because they believe individuals will add value (usually specific in nature) and are prepared to reward (through salaries, bonuses etc.) the perceived value. It is therefore important for you as an individual to be very clear about your ability to add value where it matters to the organization. You also need to identify where in the organization's chain of activities you will add the most value, and how to measure the value you add to the organization.

At some point in an organization's lifetime, changes may be required in order to meet demands. It may also be necessary to change the service or solution offerings in order to optimize profits or position the company for better growth. As a result, it is important that you understand not only where you are on the value chain, but how to move up the value chain. This movement on the value chain can be either across the chain of activities or up a given chain. For example, you may move across the value chain by moving from a support activity to a primary activity. You can do this by simply acquiring some new skill level or identifying a role where your expertise is required in the primary activity. You could also move up the value chain vertically by growing your depth of skills and knowledge along a given value adding activity. For example, you could acquire skills that move you from being the sorting personnel (technical role) to being the supervisor (managerial role) in charge of all sorting and tagging personnel. You may move from being the IT personnel (technical role) to being the head of the Information Technology team (managerial/leadership role).

Moving up the value chain (either across or vertically) is an essential requirement because at some point the organization perceives individuals not moving up the chain as being involved with wasteful activities, or simply not contributing notably to the value chain. This is usually true because if a person is truly adding value within the chain, opportunities will open up for them to move up. A person who does not add value might be asked to leave the organization. A department that does not add value might be shut down and certain individuals fired.

As a potential employee, it is essential that you understand the value chain of the company you are interviewing with and know where your expertise, skill or knowledge will be required. As an employee you need to understand your employer's value chain and how you can best contribute to it. You need to know what is considered value by the company within the chain. You must *show* that you understand what 'value' means to an employer/customer, and also show how you can effectively contribute to creating or producing that value. There, my friends, lies the key to your employability.

Finally, it is important to move up the value chain because with each move you provide more value and get better remuneration and compensation. This is the key to getting promoted faster, getting paid more, and even starting and running your own business effectively. It is the key that stands you out as a problem solver in the marketplace.

THIS IS COMMON SENSE

1. Every employer/customer has a value chain.

2. Employers/customers will give you the job if you offer a solution that will add value to their value chain.

3. In order to add value, you must understand what the employer/customer considers 'value.'

4. You must fit in the value chain of an employer/customer before you can add value.

5. For you to get more rewards, get promoted and earn more money, you must move up the value chain.

6. For you to move up the value chain you must increase the value you add to the value chain of an employer/customer. If you are not adding value, you will not earn more rewards. Even if you are earning rewards now, it will not be so for long.

ACTION EXERCISES

1. Write down the value chain of your employer/customer clearly.

2. Write down how and where (primary or support activity) you fit in the value chain of your employer/customer.

3. Write down a plan of how you will move up the value chain of your employer/customer to increase your earnings within a given time frame, for example within one year.

Chapter Nine

GIVE THEM WHAT THEY WANT

Give and take is what makes life easy. A farmer that wants to eat bread sends yam to the baker.

- Nigerian proverb

When you apply for or take up a job, you probably know what you're looking for. You want a company you love, great co-workers, great rewards and incentives, a culture where you fit in and, most importantly, you want to love what you'll be doing. But do you ever consider what the employer/customer is looking for in its solution provider? When employers or customers talk to you they want to know who you are, what you have to offer and why they should hire you as a solution provider.

If you are a prospective candidate, what you have to offer may not be what a prospective employer/customer wants. If you already have a job, what you are presently offering may not be meeting your employer's expectation. Employers/customers often expect more from employees than the employees think they should give.

No matter what industry you want to work in, your chances of getting hired or getting ahead of the pack depend on a number of important things. With competition for new jobs at an all-time high, you must have the skills employers are targeting. From the ability to lead to the willingness to wear multiple hats around the office, employers today seek workers with a variety of skills. People are their most valuable asset. Employers/customers know that people with the right knowledge, skills and expertise can provide astounding solutions that would do wonders for their business and lives. They want people who can provide solutions that will drive their business forward, or help them achieve whatever goals they desire.

There are two types of abilities needed to solve the problems of employers or customers. Whether your job falls under primary or support activities in a company's value chain, you need both types of abilities. The first is what we call the **primary ability**. This is the technical knowledge, skill or expertise required to solve a problem. For instance, if an employer/customer has an IT problem that needs IT network engineers, you have to possess knowledge in that area to be able to solve it. The primary skill is the first qualifying criterion you need to meet to be considered a problem solver to a prospective employer/customer.

The second is what we call the **supportive ability**. In addition to the relevant technical knowledge or skills required to perform required tasks, an employer/customer looks for intangible qualities that can help their company or project run smoothly and successfully. This supportive quality is what stands you out when your colleague or every other candidate has the same level of expertise as you. The supportive ability can give you the edge you need in getting a job. It can get you to be paid more. It can get you promoted faster. It can get customers to prefer your solutions over those of others.

Let's take a look at some of these supportive abilities that will help you stand out from the crowd and improve your chances of getting ahead in your work in today's technologically advanced and fast-paced workplace.

ABILITY TO EXECUTE

When an employer/customer hires you they are looking for a solution provider to a key problem or set of problems. Solving these problems is the objective of hiring you. Your employer/customer specifies this objective or objectives when you are given the job. Accomplishing these objectives first will count more than any other contributions you might make.

The solutions you will provide by achieving your critical objectives are valuable; this is why your employer is willing to pay. You are to start producing results as soon as you hit the ground. It would be a major mistake to fall short of achieving your critical objective. Hence, I must advise that if you are not passionate about solving the problems your prospective employer offers to hire you for, do not take the job. If you take the job and fail to perform, or if you perform below expectation, you're sure to get fired. Make sure you know what results your employer expects from you (sales targets, brand growth, quality control metrics, production quotas, customer retention rate etc.), exactly what tasks you should be doing, in what order you should do them and how long you should take, and how well you're expected to complete each task.

You have to understand the critical objective in order to avoid a scenario where you get off course from the key problem you are to solve. Here are a few questions you can ask yourself to help you clearly define your critical primary objective: What is my critical objective? Why is it a critical objective? Who does it impact? How does it help in achieving the overall goal of my employer? How do I know I have achieved it? When is it due?

GOING THE EXTRA MILE

The first and most important question on the minds of employers and customers is 'Can you provide the solution we seek?' The next most important question is 'How far can you go to ensure we get and exceed the results we need?' or 'How much more can you offer?' In the Bible, Jesus Christ advises: "If someone forces you to go one mile, go with him two miles." You need to do more than is required. The distance between someone who achieves their goals and those who spend their lives and careers merely following, is the extra mile. In order to gain an employer's/customer's confidence, you must be willing to go above and beyond what is typically required of you on the job. The people that get hired more easily and ultimately succeed are those that show an eagerness to do whatever needs doing, not just what's in their job description.

Most people do just what is asked of them. Doing your job and your job only is not enough. With everyone else doing just enough to keep a job, going the extra mile sets you out as the go-to person for solutions when it counts most. When you take on assignments and projects that fall outside your normal responsibilities, you expand your skills and explore new avenues for professional growth. Every time you take on a new responsibility you promote yourself. You eventually rise to the level of the responsibility you are willing to accept.

A certain friend of mine made it her responsibility to know more about her work than her job description required. She would take on more responsibilities and assignments. She made it her duty to continually get relevant knowledge and skills in areas that were not necessarily part of her critical objective. The result of her going the extra mile is that everyone at her office now sees her as the go-to person when there is a problem. This positioning has enabled her rise significantly in her career. You will only rise to the degree to which you solve problems.

Being a good employee is okay, but being a great employee is even better. A good employee gets the job done. A great employee rises up to the occasion and gets the job done in spite of their workload, seeming tight schedule and unexpected changes in priorities. A great employee takes initiative. By taking initiative, you show that you are not someone who simply meets the criteria of a job description, but one who goes above and beyond what is required to help your employer/customer succeed. Employers/customers look for great employees, pay them more and promote them faster. As Wayne Dyer says, "It's never crowded along the extra mile." Few people go the extra mile where there is outstanding success; these are the great problem solvers.

WORK SMART AND WORK HARD

Working smart means you are up to date with the latest technology, keeping your skills and professional knowledge current, and continually searching for improvements in productivity, efficiency and profitability. Working smart helps you get more work done in less time while producing better results.

Of course, good old-fashioned hard work is always needed no matter how smartly you work. There is simply no substitute for hard work. Although smart work seems to be the preference of employers/customers today, they still want to see that you are dedicated to your job, that you put in the extra effort and multitask when necessary. Employers look for diligence and expect you to be able to avoid distractions and focus on generating solutions to seemingly insurmountable problems.

Ultimately, it pays to work hard on the objectives assigned to you. In the Bible, the book of Proverbs puts it this way: "Do you know a hard-working man? He shall be successful and stand before kings."

BE DEPENDABLE

Employers/customers search for employees who can be depended upon consistently to get the job done quickly and well. An employer needs to be able to count on you to show up on time and do the work you are being paid to do. You are expected to come to work on time, work until at least closing time, and complete your assignments when they are due, or earlier, with excellence. You are expected to demonstrate your commitment to the job and show that you take your work seriously.

You show dependability by taking personal ownership of all aspects of your job, including being on time, dressing and working in a professional manner and demonstrating a high level of commitment. Employers/customers like dependable employees who set and maintain clear expectations.

BE SELF-MOTIVATED

Employers want people who are self-motivated. Self-motivated people are highly productive, and their maintenance cost (in terms of managing them) is lower because they produce more. While it's okay for you to be externally motivated by your employer, employers appreciate and seek people that create their own motivation. It makes a huge difference having an employee who possesses an inner drive to organize their work and achieve objectives versus one who needs constant guidance to perform day to day activities.

Here are four simple ways you can motivate yourself: first, find your "Why." Find the reason why you do what you do, a strong reason that makes you get out of bed every day. Money shouldn't be your reason. A powerful "why" is stronger than money. The money you earn is for that "why". Your "why" can be to provide for your family, or being able to go on wonderful vacations and buy whatever you desire, or helping other people. Whatever it is, focus on achieving it and let it drive your every action. Secondly, create a vision of who you want to be, and then live in that picture as if it were already true. It sounds ridiculous but if you think and behave the way you would if you were a very successful person, you will find that you feel motivated to act like a top performer.

Thirdly, talk positively to yourself. Yes, life can be hard sometimes so you need to talk to yourself. As soon as you wake up, tell yourself that you have greatness within and you can achieve your goals. No matter what happened yesterday, today is a new day and you are moving closer to your goal. Speaking positive words to yourself shuts down any negative conversation that may want to arise in your mind. Take some time during your day to say positive words to yourself any time you find negative thoughts creeping into your mind. Another way to do this is to write a short speech to yourself. This speech should highlight everything great about you. Focus on your strengths, why you are good at your job, and what you like about yourself. Read it to yourself whenever you feel down. The fourth thing you can do to motivate yourself is to read a motivational quote or book.

Employers look for employees whose level of self-motivation shows that they will not require much 'hand-holding,' to tackle the expected obstacles that arise in day to day business interactions. Many employees today settle for doing what is required of them —just the right amount of work to justify receiving a wage. While this may seem reasonable to most, and even the right thing to do for some, it's not what self-motivated people do. Self-motivated employees do more.

121

They are enthusiastic and dedicated, and they drive themselves to achieve more.

Your level of enthusiasm affects the way you do your work. But you can't be enthusiastic and dedicated if you don't enjoy your work. This is why, as an employee or a potential one, you should do work you're passionate about. While money is a great motivator, don't settle for just that. Think of a higher purpose. See yourself as being a passionate problem solver providing valuable solutions for organizations and customers; money will always follow.

When you find yourself excited rather than terrified about solving a problem, you know you're on the right track. Self-motivated people know that their value to an employer/customer lies in solving problems. They know that their value to an employer/customer increases when they go beyond what is expected of them. When you are motivated you will be enthusiastic about what you do. When you work with consistent enthusiasm, you produce better results because your drive is high.

BE CRUCIAL TO A POSITIVE BOTTOM LINE

If you want to be valuable to your employer/customer, then you need to contribute positively to their bottom line. In other words, you need to help them make or save money, or help them achieve their purpose. Otherwise, it's not worth it to the company to keep you around. Think about profits all the time. Make a concerted effort to connect to what it is that makes your company money, and focus on the talents and skills that you have that will contribute to those things. Focus on those items that use your time and resources most effectively so that you connect back to the bottom line.

Focus on the work you do that adds value to your employer or customer. You achieve success by producing value. You don't get paid a lot of money just for showing up at your job; you get paid a lot for your ability to repeatedly increase your employer's revenues or decrease the cost of running their business, thereby raising profits. As business philosopher Jim Rohn puts it: "You don't get paid for the hour. You get paid for the value you bring to the hour."

You must take time to learn and understand how your work impacts on the bottom line. Measure and quantify it if possible. If you are a lawyer, see your contribution to the bottom line as the impeccable legal service that limits your employer's exposure to unwarranted liability. If you are a quality control expert, see your contribution to the bottom line as ensuring customer satisfaction through your in-depth product inspections that catch flaws in products before they leave the plant. As an administrator your impact on the bottom line is the efficient and professional manner with which you handle administrative details, thereby enabling executives focus effectively on their strengths. If you are a customer service officer, see your contribution to the bottom line as ensuring customer loyalty through the professional and effective way you provide solutions to customer enquiries and complaints. Whatever work you do, make sure you can articulate how it helps the bottom line.

About five years ago in my organization, management was worried about different areas where we had cash leakages. It was surprising to note that two of the areas where we had the highest leakage were in the indiscriminate use of paper for printing, and telephone costs that had no bearing on the company's business. Unbelievably, these wasteful expenses made up at least five percent of the recurrent costs. Imagine management's disappointment after investigations were carried out and information obtained on the utilization pattern by employees.

Simply by asking employees to reuse paper for printing draft proposals and other documents that require editing, money was saved on paper purchases. Further still, simply ensuring that most of the work of editing by supervisors was done in soft copy also helped reduce our costs. Getting supervisors to edit on soft copy meant that only one draft copy printing would be required, which could also serve as the office copy. Not only was money saved on paper purchase, but a lot else was saved on toner expenses and maintenance of the printers and copiers.

Let us imagine that the idea to reduce these costs had come from the staff member that had been charged with photocopying and printing. Don't you think that management would have taken notice of him? No matter what your job description says, if you have a mindset of either making your company more money or reducing their costs, someone will eventually notice you and the reward will come when you least expect it. More importantly, you will be positioning yourself for a time when a problem solver will be required. Make it a habit to solve problems that contribute positively to the bottom line of your employer/customer.

BE AN EFFECTIVE TIME INVESTOR

Employers are interested in people who invest their time in providing solutions. Benjamin Franklin's statement that "time is money" captures the importance of your time to your employers/customers. The most valuable commodity you have is your own time. Employers/customers do not only pay for your ability to solve problems but also for the time you spend doing so. Employers expect you not to waste the time you are paid for. They need you to solve problems during that time.

Often, there are no greater timewasters in the workplace than your colleagues. There are the colleagues who love to gossip, spread rumours and just chat away on the employer's time. In some cases, there is the office flirt. Besides colleagues, there is also the internet, with Facebook, Twitter, Instagram, YouTube and other social media platforms and applications that can suck you in and make you waste valuable time. All your work hours should be spent actually working.

Here are three simple ways you can avoid distractions and stay focused at work:

-Plan ahead. Plan what you want to achieve in your workday before you begin the day. Write down what things need to get done or what must be accomplished. Setting goals can help you stay on track.

-Work offline. Most disruptions at work come from email, social networks and cell phones. So for tasks that don't involve the internet, disconnect the internet service. Limit time spent on social media too. Consider turning off notifications for your email or social media accounts. Better still, when it's time to work put your phone on silent and turn off your data connection. You can "like" your friend's picture later. Set a particular time for checking email. If your work does not require regular email correspondence, don't open your mail immediately you get to the office. Start work on your planned goals for the day.

-Start on your tasks immediately. Once you get to the office, begin executing your planned tasks immediately. Leave the morning chitchat with colleagues. To make this even more effective, you can come in thirty minutes earlier than your colleagues so they meet you working. This gives the impression you have a lot to do, and leaves no room for long morning chats.

You need to place value on your time because your time is your life. If you do not value your time then you do not value yourself. Employers are not looking for loafers or drones. They want people who understand the value of time and act with urgency to solve problems in today's fast-paced workplace. Problem solvers do not waste time on unproductive activities.

Time is the currency of life. How you utilise it determines your future rewards. You are either wasting it, spending it or investing it. Fools waste it; the mediocre spends it; but the wise invest it. Rather than waste or just spend your time, ensure that your time counts. Invest it, even when at play. A problem solver consciously invests his or her time, and will eventually be rewarded handsomely when the investment matures.

BE A LEADER

People with leadership ability are able to lead themselves and others to solve problems; this is why employers/customers value this quality. John C. Maxwell describes a leader as "one who knows the way, goes the way, and shows the way." Former U.S Secretary Colin Powell simply states that "Leadership is solving problems."

The mark of a leader is that he or she accepts complete responsibility for the situation. A true leader does not whine and complain when problems and difficulties arise. Leaders do not give excuses. They take responsibility for outcomes and hold themselves accountable for the results they get. They take necessary action to solve problems. Ultimately, they inspire and motivate others to higher levels of performance. The ability to lead will definitely cause you to stand out. Learn to lead.

There are a number of actions you can take to develop yourself into a leader. But we recommend you start with these two powerful steps. First, discipline yourself to follow through and complete every assignment and responsibility given to you on schedule and with excellence. After you are done with your assignment, ask for more. Go where expectations and demand to perform are high. Become a task master to yourself. You earn the right to lead others when you are first able to lead yourself. Secondly, choose a successful leader you respect and model your actions after that person. If they are in your environment, observe them and ask for mentorship. If you are not in the same environment with them you can read their books or biographies.

BE A THINKER

Besides particular technical skills, what employers/customers want most are people who can think clearly, creatively and critically. Thomas Edison said, "Five percent of the people think; ten percent of the people think they think; and the other eighty-five percent would rather die than think." Becoming part of the five percent that think makes you outstanding. Being able to think through and creatively provide solutions is a highly desirable skill if you must provide value. We discussed this skill extensively in Chapter Four. You can read it up again.

BE HONEST

An employer expects you to be honest. Your employer must know that they can trust you to be honest about your performance on any assignment. For example, if you know you cannot meet a deadline you need to let your employer know in advance so they can mobilize more hands to help if need be. You should also be honest in the sense of being ethical in your practice.

YOU HAVE TO KNOW

For you to give employers what they want you have to get to know what they want. Here are a few questions you can ask to gain insight: Who is your employer? Why are they here? Where are they going? What solution do they need? Why do they want the solution? When do they want the solution? How do you intend to contribute to your employer's purpose? How do you plan to provide the solution? What level of performance do they want?

THIS IS COMMON SENSE

1. Employers/customers have goals they want to achieve.

2. They need you to solve key problems so they can achieve their goals.

3. You need to understand their goals.

4. Your job is to solve problems that will help them achieve these goals.

5. You need to have both primary and supportive abilities in order for you to solve their problems and help them achieve their goals.

6. You need to invest time in learning and mastering these

128

abilities.

ACTION EXERCISES

1. Identify and write down the key goal of your employer or customer. The questions in the 'You Need to Know' section will help you in this exercise.

2. Write down your primary and supportive abilities that will enable you solve their problem.

3. If you don't have the right abilities, write down actions you can take to develop them, and then take action.

Chapter Ten

GENERATE WILLINGNESS TO PAY (WTP): CREATE AND APPROPRIATE VALUE

When the right hand washes the left and the left washes the right, both hands become clean.

- Nigerian proverb

Chapter 9 focused on what employers/customers expect from you as an employee, but this chapter focuses on what you as an employee would like to earn and how to motivate employers/customers to pay what you ask.

Here is a thought-provoking conversation:

Kelechi: *Ayodele, I intend to look for another job and leave this company. I am thinking of getting married in four years and my salary has not been increased in the three years since I got employed here. This company does not want to increase my salary.*

Ayodele:*Why don't you set a goal to double or possibly triple your income within the next three years in readiness for your wedding?*

Kelechi: *That is not possible, especially in this company. They are too stingy and will not pay well.*

Ayodele: *Are you sure about this?*

Kelechi: *I am quite sure.*

Ayodele:*That is quite strange. Does this mean everyone earns the same salary in the company?*

Kelechi: *No, of course not! I believe Haruna, my well-respected supervisor, should be earning at least three or four times my salary.*

Ayodele:*This means that the company is willing to pay someone higher — twice your salary and more —but not you. Why is that?*

Kelechi: *I guess you are right; I have been on the same job for the past three years. I do basically what I get paid for. Haruna, on the other hand, has been promoted at least twice and he very well deserved those promotions. He is versatile, works smart and always does   more than his fair share of work.*

Ayodele:*So it is not the company that is unwilling to pay you more. You just have not done enough to create the willingness for them to pay you more.*

Kelechi: *I see what you mean…*

In ordinary terms, Willingness to Pay (WTP) is your ability to demonstrate so much value that employers/customers willingly accept to pay the price that you have set. The concept of willingness to pay is usually associated with payment for goods and services. However, it is very important to consistently practise, as an individual, ways to increase willingness to pay on any service you render. You can practise increasing willingness to pay during an interview for a job, on your job, and all through your career.

A conscious practice of increasing willingness to pay is what makes a problem solver stand out. It is what helps people to get high paying jobs. It is what helps some people progress more rapidly than others in the marketplace. This concept puts you in good stead even before you are employed, and sustains you through your career when you consciously put it to practice. Let's take a closer look at this concept.

OFFER VALUE

Pere and Ebiye worked for their father whose business was farming. Ebiye, the younger brother, had earned greater rewards consistently for a period of time. Pere, the older brother, could not understand why his younger brother was rewarded more. He felt that this was his right as the older brother. Tired of this unfair treatment, Pere walks up to his father one day and asks for an explanation.

The father says, "I'll explain, but first, go to Owei's farm and see if they have any juveniles of cat fish for sale. We need some for the new fish pond."

Pere gets into the car, drives to Owei's farm and soon returns with an answer, "Yes, they have five thousand they can sell to us."

The father then asks, "What's the price?"

Pere replies, "I'll find out."

And off he goes again.

He returns with the answer: "The juveniles are N25 each."

The father asks, "Can they deliver the juveniles tomorrow?"

Pere replies, "I'll go find out."

And off he goes, for the third time.

Soon enough, Pere returns with the answer: "Owei's farm said they can deliver the juveniles tomorrow."

The father then says to Pere, "Just wait a while, watch and listen." He then calls Ebiye, the younger brother. He says, "Go to Ebi's Farm and find out if they have any juveniles for sale. We need some for our new fish pond."

Ebiye drives off and soon returns with the answer: "They do have juveniles. The price for five thousand juveniles is N25 each. If we are buying up to ten thousand juveniles they sell at N22 each, and they can deliver tomorrow. I instructed them to deliver five thousand juveniles unless they heard otherwise from us before the end of the day. I also got an agreement with Mr. Ebi that if we want the extra five thousand juveniles we would pay N20 for each."

Their father then looked at Pere and asked, "Do you understand now?" With a look of understanding on his face, Pere replied, "I understand clearly."

The younger son offered exceptional value. He went beyond and above expectations, saving time and money. On the other hand, the older brother did only what he was told and nothing more. He did not provide any added value. Are you offering added value, or are you just showing up?

The money you earn will ultimately be in exact proportion to the need for what you do, your ability to do it and the difficulty there will be in replacing you. You will always be compensated adequately if you offer what people need or value.

With cases where there are limited vacancies and most of the candidates have the right qualifications, what makes the difference

133

between the successful candidates and the rest of the qualified bunch will be the ability to create, show and appropriate value during the interview. If the interview is in an engineering firm, for instance, you will stand out by dressing well (candidates for engineering positions tend to dress casually), being well-groomed and, above all, knowing about the company and their current challenges. Nothing makes an employer gladder than to know that, apart from your technical capability, you understand quite clearly how your presence in the firm adds to the bottom line and creates efficiency while improving the top line and brand quality, and not just as mere rhetoric or textbook cliché.

If an engineer knows a bit of finance and understands the effect of accounts receivable (money expected) on the fortunes of the company, he then is able to translate in concrete terms how his input to delivering on time will cut down the accounts receivable days, thereby increasing the cash available to the company. Over and above the technical competence required, such candidates will be noticed.

A story comes to mind very readily. We were interviewing some candidates for the position of network engineers, to be trained on the job. We had a lot of candidates waiting to be interviewed, some qualified (based on their resumes) and others not so qualified. All through the interviews, most of the interviewees repeated the same cliché: 'I am hard working, I am effective, I can work with little or no supervision.'

After each session with a candidate, we asked if they had any questions. One candidate stood out; he did not have a first class degree, and neither was he the best in terms of engineering knowledge, but he got a job for a role he had not been interviewing for. How did he achieve that? While others asked how long it would take to become a senior engineer, and other similar questions, the young man simply made a statement. 'Sir," he said, "while I was preparing for this interview I did a bit of research on the company, and I realized that with most of your customers there is a bit of a challenge with project management as the customers I researched all rate you high in engineering knowledge but complained about the delivery timeline. I have thought through what some of these challenges are and here are my thoughts and possible recommendations for improvement."

He touched a pain point of the organization, and he even came to the table with possible solutions. Today, he is one of the best project managers around. He created a space for himself and a willingness to pay for his service in the hearts of the entire interview panel, because he came to the table and connected by creating value. This is what we call the 'Joseph model' for interviewees.

The Joseph model is derived from the Bible, from the story of a man named Joseph who got an opportunity to show he could solve the problem of a country. When he was brought before the king, Joseph got to know his pain; he understood and then interpreted the problem. Being a problem solver by habit, without being asked, he immediately proceeded to articulate the solution to the problem. He mapped out a strategic blueprint for solving the problem, and was instantly given an appointment so he could execute the plan. Of course, the office he was appointed to as a result came with great rewards.

When you go for interviews, what do you know about the company you are interviewing with? What are their pain points? Do you know and understand them? If you do, what can you do about it? What strategic blueprint can you offer for their problem?

UNDERSTAND YOUR VALUE

One thing we have learned is that everyone has value, but not everyone understands the value they possess or can bring to the table. Because of this lack of understanding, they may never be able to position themselves to generate the willingness to pay in the hearts of employers/customers. Merriam-Webster defines 'understanding' as the knowledge and ability to judge a particular situation or subject; a mental grasp; the power of comprehending, especially the capacity to apprehend general relations of particulars. There is a great difference between knowing and understanding. You can know so much about something and yet not really understand it. Your ability to comprehend, apprehend and come to a mental grasp of what value you possess and can offer is the beginning of creating value.

The first step in creating willingness to pay is understanding what value you have or can create, or what value stands you out beyond the average person. This will require some stock-taking and introspection, and sometimes asking very difficult questions of yourself and of people who know you. A good start will be to carry out a Johari Window assessment.[8] (Note that this is not necessarily the primary reason for a Johari Window assessment. This assessment is primarily for self-awareness, personal development and team communication.) This helps you to put your strengths into perspective.

Most people dwell on their weaknesses to the detriment of their strengths, and therefore never excel. Focus on your strengths while working on your weaknesses, knowing full well that even your best improved-on weakness cannot be as strong as your smallest strength. Therefore, spend more time improving on your strengths, and provide avenues to work on your weakness to better them without beating yourself over the head. There is a saying popularly attributed to

136

Albert Einstein: "Everybody is a genius. But if you judge a fish by its ability to climb a tree, it will live its whole life believing that it is stupid."

The main job of the fish is to find its water and not to beat itself over the head for not being able to climb a tree as a monkey would. Even if by dint of hard work the fish is able to climb a tree, a baby monkey will still trounce it without effort. The question is what is your water? Sometimes you may also need to ask where your water is. To create willingness to pay, you need to be in your water and know it. Your genius is in finding your water and learning to be the best swimmer. If you have a natural affinity for sales, then spend time developing your sales skills and techniques and don't knock yourself down for not being the best system designer. When the system is fully designed it will need to be sold — you will shine better selling the designed system rather than killing yourself trying to be the best system designer.

When you consistently get affirmation for what you do, then you will have understood your value. In the late 80s and early 90s, there were very few comedians in Nigeria who understood their value. Some did comedy out of passion but were not validated because they never really placed value on what they did. Most took it as hobby, something they enjoyed doing. However, comedians like Ali Baba soon came on the scene. Ali Baba took his time to understand his unique strength and also the value that comedy and humour bring to the populace, and he became a household name for it. Now, comedy is a major industry in Nigeria with great earning potential in and out of the country. Comedians are now valued and affirmed. They know they bring value, and they ensure the people know this too.

It is important to understand that your value is always within a context. This brings to mind the question of where your water is. For example Ali Baba, who is a top earning comedian in Nigeria, would most likely not be reckoned with by Americans for his jokes because his material and humour are contextualized for the Nigerian environment. In the same vein Chris Rock, who is a famous stand-up comedian in America, may not strike the same chord as Bovi, another Nigerian comedian, in Nigeria. However, a Bovi will do excellently well in a crowd of Nigerians in Houston, Texas, because they understand his context.

If Ali Baba insists on pleasing the American crowd, his best will hardly match the worst of Chris Rock. However, in Nigeria or with a Nigerian audience anywhere in the world, Ali Baba is a star of no mean repute. Understanding your value also involves understanding the context. We can extend the fish example as follows: If you ask a monkey, a fish and a zebra to climb a tree, the monkey appears a genius. However, switch the context to swimming and the fish is king. If the arena is the Serengeti and the contest is a 100m race, then the Zebra will have won before any of the other contestants even start. Therefore, understand your value, but more appropriately, understand it within a given value chain or context.

SELL THE RIGHT PERCEPTION

Perception is a projection of your beliefs at the subconscious level, which then manifests as your reality. If you perceive yourself as not possessing much value that is what you believe; and because that is what you believe, you will sell yourself short to your employer or customer.

This brings to mind an experience with a young man during an interview session. The young man was asked how much he would like to be paid. His poor self-perception spoke when he showed he had no clue as to the value he had and the worth of this value. This is how our conversation went:

Interviewer: How much do you want to be paid?

Candidate: (In a low tone) Sixty thousand naira.

Interviewer: Did I hear you say sixty thousand naira?

Candidate: Fifty thousand naira.

(Just to ascertain what he'd said, he was asked again.)

Interviewer: Did you mean fifty thousand naira?

(Not sure about the motive for asking, the candidate became desperate.)

Candidate: Forty thousand naira.

This candidate was selling a wrong perception of himself. His inconsistency showed that he perceived himself as not having much value to offer. Because of this perception he did not see himself as worth a high figure, and so he sold himself short to a potential employer. If anybody has a perception like this young man's they will ultimately create one of these two realities: no offer of employment, or employment with very low pay for the value they will provide.

During a different interview session, we met with a candidate who was fresh out of university. Unlike other candidates, she exuded self-confidence and had done her homework. At the end of the interview, she requested twice our standard salary for fresh graduates. Even though we had lots of other qualified candidates more than willing to accept our compensation package, the members of the panel all considered discussing with the HR director to see if there was any way we could review our remuneration package just for her. We all felt sure we would be losing a major asset if we allowed her walk out without an offer. This candidate had never worked with us and so we had no way of judging her work, except by asking her previous employer with whom she had worked as an intern. However, because she was able to sell her perception she got a whole team of experienced interviewers thinking about making exceptions in spite of the difficulty this would present. Your interview sessions should leave your interviewers feeling that they must have you or they would have lost a gem.

For you to sell the right perception, you must catch attention —the right way. Do you dress shabbily for interviews or do you have a power suit and cologne for that special meeting? Do you walk sloppily and carry the weight of despondency on your face when you walk into a meeting? Or do you exude confidence, energy and passion?

Apart from interview sessions, every opportunity to showcase your talent should be exploited in style (not necessarily in a flamboyant or arrogant manner) to show that you really have great value to offer. Arrogance will not work. We can tell you from experience about someone who had the competence for a position but was turned down because he exuded arrogance. Perception, they say, is reality. Your perception of yourself will ultimately become your reality, and so you have to make sure you are selling the right perception of yourself —as a problem solver offering great value.

APPROPRIATE YOUR VALUE

One of the problems with would-be employees is that most of them have no idea what they want, what they are about (the value they carry) and what value is expected of them by the would-be employer. The employer is not doing you a favour, and neither are you doing the employer a favour —value is simply being exchanged on both sides. This brings us to the concept of appropriating your value. A typical example is in the software industry where an idea is sold at a given value and no one complains of the cost because the value is seen and felt by users.

The average cost to manufacture a computer is less than one third of its retail price, yet people buy computers without complaining about the cost. Nike footwear costs a lot less to produce than their retail price, yet Nike has die-hard fans and followers. Apple has created a whole community of ardent fans and aficionados for all things Apple. Even with prices twice the competition's, these Apple lovers are more than willing to pay and are effusive about the value they get from Apple.

The key lesson is that Apple, and others like it, do not merely create value; they actively seek ways to appropriate the value from their creation and value addition. The same principle can be found in the fashion industry. The average cost of production of designer bags and shoes is much less than 30 percent of their retail price. Yet, there is a whole class of people who will pay willingly for these products. In the same industry, items of comparable value are priced at less than a 20 percent margin (profit). What is the difference? It's the ability to appropriate value created.

In order to be able to appropriate value, you need to know what is considered value by the employer/customer, and by which customer segment. A good example is the bottled water business in Nigeria. At the beginning, provision of cold water to travellers was seen as the value. However, water is commodity and not much value could be appropriated. Some people discovered that value could be created by properly bottling the water. The margin on bottled water more than quadrupled as a result of appropriate packaging. If the packaging is not attractive, distinct and appealing, the likelihood is that you have lost value. You might be making a good profit, but it could be more.

Also, to appropriate value you need to go the extra mile to understand what is really important to your employers/customers. What you consider value may not necessarily be value to other people. However, when you are certain that what you are offering is great value to employers/customers, do not be afraid to request or demand the equivalent reward for this value. Do not be afraid or ashamed to appropriate the value you created. There is no moral high ground in not appropriating value. Do not leave value on the table without getting your due.

ACTIVATE WILLINGNESS TO PAY

In summation, to activate Willingness To Pay you need to know and understand your value, and know the right place of exchange for the value. You need to sell the right perception when you find the right place of exchange, and get value for your offer.

THIS IS COMMON SENSE

1. Employers/customers are always willing to pay whatever price you ask if they perceive your solutions to be highly valuable.

2. You have to know what top value is to employers/customers.

3. You should then offer this value to them.

4. You have to understand and believe in the value you are offering.

5. You have to confidently project the worth of your value.

6. You can then ask for the reward for the value you created.

ACTION EXERCISES

1. Write down what your employer/customer will term a 'must have' value.

2. Write down what you think this value would be worth to your employer/customer.

3. Write down how you can sell yourself as a provider of this value to make employers/customers pay you the amount of money you will ask.

Note

[8] *http://en.wikipedia.org/wiki/Johari_window (For a Johari Window assessment online you can go to http://kevan.org/johari)*

Chapter Eleven

LEARN TO NEGOTIATE AND GET GOOD AT IT

The heap of yams you will reap depends upon the number of mounds you have ploughed.

- Nigerian proverb

Let us start this chapter by making this categorical statement: Life is a constant wheel of negotiations, and to get ahead you need to be good at it. Most people engage in negotiation on a daily basis without even knowing it. Negotiation can be impromptu. For example, if a friend wants you to do something urgent for them and you are in a hurry to go somewhere, you might negotiate for a convenient time. As an entrepreneur seeking investors, you approach a bank and you start a negotiation by putting forward your best proposal, and the bank gets back to you. This may go back and forth till you arrive at a negotiated position. In your job interview, you are negotiating —the company wants the best personnel to fill a position and at the right price. You, the interviewee, want a place of work that will provide a living wage and above. You might also have some other objectives, like a good work environment, a job that allows for a fair work-life balance, a family friendly environment etc.

Negotiation is at the centre of our daily existence —either on a personal informal basis or as part of our work or business. It could be as simple as making and receiving your request, or as complex as involving an entire nation. Whatever the situation, you don't get what you deserve; you get what you negotiate. It is imperative that, as individuals who wish to get ahead in life, we recognise opportunities for negotiation; and as much as possible we should be prepared and put into use some basic principles to enable us get as much out of the situations as possible.

WHAT DOES NEGOTIATION REALLY MEAN?

In order to provide some context and perspective, it is important to state what negotiation is not. Negotiation is not an opportunity to crush the other party. Negotiation is not about ridiculing the other party to prove a point and, above all, it is not about having your way at all costs. Negotiation is based on objectives and expected outcomes in a given context or situation. It is a measure of what is important and what is considered value and valuable. Success in a negotiation is about striking a deal that meets the core expectations of the parties involved.

For example, in an interview, the company's major objective usually is to employ the best fit (based on skills, attitude, knowledge etc.) for a position while ensuring that the pay package and other benefits are within a reasonable range which the company can reasonably and realistically pay given their context. For the interviewee, objectives vary including any or all of the following: a conducive environment, a great brand, above industry average emolument, family-friendly workplace, training and learning opportunity, job security etc. What is important for both parties is to find a space where their objectives and expectations match, and in the process, where necessary, trade-offs are made to accommodate each other's needs.

A close relation once told of how he got a job offer with a company and they wanted him to relocate from Port Harcourt in Rivers State to Lagos. This relation was a newlywed and his young bride had just succeeded in getting a transfer to Port Harcourt. He did not want to have to leave his wife and move to a different state, and it would be difficult for her to get another transfer immediately. He decided the best way out was to make a trade-off. In the negotiations for his salary, he demanded a higher wage if he was to relocate to Lagos, and a bit less if the company allowed him to remain in Port Harcourt. The less pay trade-off sounded reasonable to the company. He was given the job and got to stay in Port Harcourt with his wife.

As with success in every area, it is important to know the basic principles that will enable you get the best out of the negotiation opportunities available to you. Let's take a look at these principles.

DEFINE YOUR OBJECTIVES

It is very important, perhaps the most important thing in any given negotiation, to define clearly in your mind what your objectives are, even in situations of impromptu negotiation. Without this, you will most likely either throw value away or get into a deadlock when there should be none. Objectives are not necessarily a list of must-haves. Objectives are guiding thoughts that enable you decide what is important and what is not.

Chief (Mrs.) A. Shokela was an 89-year-old widow with no children. She lived in an estate which she had inherited from her late husband. She had a gardener who had served her and her late husband for over 25 years; he had practically become her family. This gardener lived on the estate with his family.

Chief (Mrs.) A. Shokela wanted to sell the land and give the money to charity when she died, since she had no heir. Most importantly, though, she wanted whoever bought the land to ensure that the gardener and his entire family were retained and offered a job. This was a key item on her list of objectives. However, most prospective buyers she came across simply wanted the estate for its worth and were not interested in the gardener or his family. In the long run, she sold to the lowest bidder, who wanted to keep the gardener and his family on the estate.

For Chief (Mrs.) Shokela, her objective was not necessarily money but the welfare of the gardener and his family. This leads to the second principle of negotiation.

FIND OUT THE OTHER'S OBJECTIVES

You need to find out as quickly as possible, and as clearly as possible, the objective(s) of the other party or parties. Getting to know the other party's objective(s) may be quite easy in a simple personal or impromptu situation. On the other hand, it may be quite difficult and complex, for example, in very tough and protracted labour negotiations where there are myriad issues.

In a job interview, it is usually possible to find out these objectives with some research. For example, a company interviewing for the position of a quality assurance person most likely wants to improve or stabilize their product or service quality. However, beyond that, there may be specific issues around the quality that go beyond just the obvious, and the best candidate would be the one that most closely articulates what the situation is or what the anticipated solution is likely to be.

Make it your priority to discover what a win really looks like for the other person. A candidate who wishes to succeed in getting the job would do well to research about what aspects of quality (as well as other issues) are of major concern to the company. This can be obtained from articles on the company in the papers, on the internet,

147

or even through discussions with the company's customers or employees. With the information gathered you would have thought of possible solutions to these issues before the interview. This causes you to stand out.

ALWAYS HAVE A BATNA

BATNA is a term coined by Roger Fisher and William Ury in their 1981 bestseller, *Getting to Yes: Negotiating Without Giving In*. It stands for 'Best Alternative To Negotiated Agreement.' In other words, it is the best you can do if the other person refuses to negotiate with you —if they tell you to 'go jump in a lake!' or 'get lost!' So this is not necessarily your ideal outcome —unless if your ideal outcome is something you can get without the cooperation of the other person. It is the best you can do without them.

Let's say for instance you were offered a job by a certain company, with a monthly salary of N150,000. Your current job pays N100,000 monthly. However, to take this new job you will need to relocate to the metropolis where your monthly recurrent cost will be about N145,000. With your present employment and in your current neighbourhood, your cost of living on a monthly basis is about N80,000. If you have an avenue to negotiate the pay package offered by the new company, you should be asking for nothing less than N165,000 in order to meet your present level of savings, or else your BATNA is your current job.

BATNAs are not always readily apparent. Fisher and Ury outline a simple process for determining your BATNA:

1. Develop a list of actions you might conceivably take if no agreement is reached;

148

2. Improve some of the more promising ideas and convert them into practical options; and

3. Select, tentatively, the one option that seems best.

ZONE OF POSSIBLE AGREEMENT (ZOPA)

This is tougher to achieve but it helps to analyze it to know where you can come to a comfortable and beneficial agreement. ZOPA allows you to know the possible zone of agreement between the partners. It also ensures that the time spent negotiating to reach an agreement is not prolonged unnecessarily.

Take this scenario: a company is only able to pay a wage/salary of N100,000 on a monthly basis based on their capacity and cash flow. You are interested in working with this company; however, you already have a job that pays you N150,000 monthly. It is instantly clear that there is no area of overlap between your expectation and how much the company can pay, no matter how much they want to have you work for them. If the option of taking a pay cut does not arise for you, then you are better off not even attempting to apply for the job because there will be no Zone of Possible Agreement.

When there is no Zone of Possible Agreement, you are said to be in a negative bargaining zone. As much as possible, it is important to get an idea of the ZOPA to ensure negotiating teams do not get into the negative bargaining zone because it usually is non-productive and leads to heated arguments and rising tempers.

WHAT IS YOUR SUCCESS?

During any negotiation, all parties intend to win. Therefore, there must be a solution that is agreeable to all. In winning, however, ensure that the other party feels good about your win. Ensure that they do not feel cheated, bullied or backed into a corner because, more often than not, there may be opportunities to negotiate again in the future, and in the indelible words of Maya Angelou, "I've learned that people will forget what you said, people will forget what you did, but people will never forget how you made them feel." Even when your objectives have been met, ensure that the other party feels fairly treated and not blackmailed.

For instance, during a recruitment process where you are the only suitable candidate the company got for the job, ensure that in your negotiation for benefits and compensation you do not appear greedy or eager to hold the company to ransom. You can give concessions that will endear you to your employer/customer from the first day and still not reduce your salary package. At the end of the day, leave the other party with a good feeling even where no agreement is possible.

Never cross the line from negotiation on objectives and principles to verbal personal attacks. If you do so you might be burning valuable bridges and ruining any chance of a relationship or future business with the other party. Even if a negotiation is not successful, leaving the other party with a good or positive feeling might cause them to recommend you to someone else, and this way you gain.

THIS IS COMMON SENSE

1. You have to negotiate to get your desired reward.

2. You have to be clear about how much you want to earn before you meet an employer/customer.

3. You have to be clear about what your employer/customer wants and what they would consider a fair deal.

4. You need to have an understanding of what your employer or customer is willing and able to pay, and how it meets your expectations.

5. You need to have a back-up plan in case you don't get the offer you are expecting.

6. You have negotiated successfully when you get the reward you want and your employer/customer still feels like they got a fair deal. Ensure they have that feeling.

ACTION EXERCISES

1. Write down what you want to get when you meet your employer/customer to negotiate.

2. Write down what your employer/customer will consider a fair deal given the solution you are offering.

3. Write down how you can give your employer/customer a fair deal and still win.

Chapter Twelve

YOU, YES YOU —YOU ARE THE ANSWER

When the rain falls on the leopard, it wets the spots on its skin but does not wash them off.

- Ashanti proverb

While talking with a friend about the rate of unemployment in the country, he mentioned the poor attitude and incompetence that he had observed in the employees of a certain company. We shared some of our experiences interviewing prospective employees.

On a certain occasion an organization wanted to hire a number of ICT engineers, and after interviewing several candidates they could not get even one fully qualified person that met all their requirements. Most of the interviewees did not even understand the basics of engineering. They were all ICT graduates. On another occasion an organization invited candidates who had applied for the position of secretary for a test. The candidates were all given a simple task of writing memos and letters. Surprisingly, some candidates did not know the format of a letter; others had no idea what a memo was. For some others their work was riddled with grammatical and spelling errors. Yet these were all graduates. The most ridiculous display of incompetence for that recruitment exercise was the candidate who sat staring at the laptop he was given for the duration of the task. When asked why he did not attempt the task he said he could not open Microsoft Word. Yet he had come to interview for a job that required computer skills.

It is amazing that at a time when information about anything can be obtained at the touch of a button, some people still live in ignorance, to their own detriment. Why would all those candidates choose not to invest some time to gain competence? After much consideration, we resolved that the real problem is not about lack of employment. It is really about employability. Some people have unwittingly put themselves in a state in which they are simply unemployable. There are countless problems to be solved, but most people cannot be given the job or the responsibility because they do not have the requisite abilities or knowledge needed. They are simply unemployable.

Many jobseekers are more concerned with how much remuneration they can get than with how much value they can offer. This focus on getting a reward without considering the solution they would offer an employer/customer is the reason most people do not take the time to invest in developing themselves. You can only get the reward you desire by providing outstanding solutions. You just have to choose to take on the right mindset. The easy thing to do is to throw your hands in the air and give up. Of course, you will have lots of reasons to justify this choice. But you have to let go of your 'reasons' and focus on providing results.

BECOME ACCOUNTABLE TO YOURSELF

The first step to reaching your goals is to stop making excuses and playing the blame game. Become accountable for and to yourself. In the book, *Executing your Strategy*, Mark Morgan, Raymond E. Levitt and William Malek give clear insight into what accountability implies. Accountability is the ability to:

· Acknowledge the truth about the results that have been created

· Accept ownership of the choices that drove the results

- Declare a path forward consisting of the choices that will be made in the future.

The popular biblical story of the prodigal son vividly illustrates the act of holding oneself accountable. In the story, the prodigal son wasted his inheritance and thereafter experienced great hardship. However, the young man came to his senses and acknowledged the reality facing him. He accepted that it was his choices that had led him to his present situation. He then made a decision about his way forward. He decided to go back to his father, ask for forgiveness and beg to be hired as a servant so he could earn a living and be responsible. He became accountable and got a much better outcome than he had hoped for. Choose to be accountable.

BECOME AND STAY DESIRABLE

I was once on a flight from Abuja to Lagos when at some point the intercom came on and a male voice thanked us for flying with the airline. Out of everything the speaker said, one sentence stood out for me because it described a distinction I've often observed in the marketplace. He said, "There are only two airlines —our airline and the others." The speaker was making a statement regarding their brand identity as the best air travel solutions provider. His point was that although other airlines were **available** they could not be compared to them —they were the best and the most **desirable** airline to fly with.

As a rule we all know the best is always more desirable than the available. This is why we are willing to pay more for product or service brands we perceive as the best. This is also true with people. We've come to observe that there are people with an identity as 'the desirable', and there are 'the others' with no such identity but who are also available. Problem solvers always stand out as the desirable. Employers/customers are always willing to pay for their services.

To become desirable, you have to take personal responsibility for developing yourself. You have to stay on a continual knowledge and skills upgrade program. Don't wait until an organization or anyone else sends you on training before you upgrade your knowledge and skills. Be the investor in your personal development. Invest in books, audio and video training programs, and attend relevant seminars to develop yourself. Some of you may have ready excuses such as, 'I am not even earning a living, so how do I get the funds to attend these trainings?' The truth is that for a mind on a quest, there is always a way. There are so many free online resources for training and self - development, such as Coursera, KHAN Academy etc. All you need to do is tap into the amazing and vast resources made available at almost no cost to you. You are the one who stands to benefit, so don't wait for someone to invest in you before you upgrade yourself. Continually work on yourself to make sure you become and remain part of the desirable instead of the available.

We were once recruiting for a company that needed a highly experienced person to head a particular unit. Among the applicants was this 50-year-old woman. Experience was a very important factor for this job so we decided to give her a chance. However, after the MD of the company, who happened to be much younger, had finished with her, the woman felt floored. She had relied on the knowledge she had acquired long ago and had stopped upgrading herself. She had experience but was out of touch with present-day practice in her field. She recounted after the interview that she could not believe someone much younger than her could take her out so easily. She admitted she had not taken responsibility for her self-development and decided she would never let that happen again. There was a time when she ranked among the best in her field. She was highly desirable then, but over the years she had unwittingly slipped into being merely 'available' by not taking responsibility for her self-development. The question you have to answer is, Are you **desirable** or are you part of 'the others' who are just **available**? Choose to be someone significant, with the identity of a desirable problem solver. Take responsibility for making yourself desirable to employers/customers.

GET CLARITY

I once walked into a supermarket to buy some items I needed. When I got to the cashier's desk I held out a N1,000 bill to pay for my items, which cost a total of N540. Almost immediately the cashier snapped, "I don't have change!", as though she was angry at me over some previous disagreement. I had to calm her down and remind her that I was her customer and she was supposed to handle the situation professionally. I told her what she should have done, with a smile — she should have given me 'other available options.'

The cashier had acted this way because she did not have clarity about her job. She was hired not just to collect the cash payments but to actually solve a problem for her employer by handling any issue that may arise during the payment process. But she was not clear about this.

Having clarity affects the way a person acts or responds to situations in life. If you are clear about what problem you are supposed to be solving, your actions will be better focused on solving that

157

problem. To get clarity, you have to think and visualize your goal, the result you want, and write it down. Goals are the vision of your expected result or future. Goals help focus your actions. Set a personal goal to establish yourself as a problem solver in your field.

You have to be clear about who you want to be seen as. You cannot take appropriate action on something that you are not clear about. What is the purpose of the solution you are offering? You need to understand clearly what problem you want to solve, for whom, and what rewards you want in exchange. You need to be clear about the value you have to offer, and you need to be clear about the right place of exchange.

TAKE ACTION

You can only get rewarded when you take action to solve problems. Until your knowledge, skills, awareness, insights and understanding are translated to action that creates solutions, they are of no value. You have to become action oriented. You can only establish yourself as a problem solver when you take action towards becoming that person. This means that whenever you think of anything that you want you should automatically think of the action that you can take to achieve it. Whenever you discover a problem that employers/customers are facing you should automatically think of the actions that you can take to solve it. Then take those actions.

The world rewards people who reach out and grab it with both hands. It rewards those who do something rather than just wish and hope and plan and pray and intend to do something someday, when everything is just right. You have to understand that everything will never be 'just right.' However, if you set a goal to solve a problem and take action toward your goal, you will begin creating the circumstances that will lead to your desired reward. Make a list of actions you must begin taking immediately to position yourself as a problem solver, and then take those actions.

YOU HAVE TO SELL YOURSELF

It is not enough that you have the needed skills and knowledge; you need to work on getting your employer/customer to have a positive perception of you. Employers/customers will only buy your problem-solving skills if you are able to sell them on YOU as the person they need to solve their problem. You have successfully sold yourself when your employer/customer develops the perception that you are the best candidate, that you are very good at what you do and that you will definitely provide the needed solution. People act and respond based on the perceptions they have. It is not what they see but what they think they see that determines how they think and act. You have to raise your credibility to the point where your employer/customer perceives that you are the right solution provider they need.

To sell yourself you need to first have content (the right solution your employer/customer needs). Secondly, but very importantly, you need to have a planned presentation. Your presentation is your packaging. Your presentation is how you sell yourself. Here are two things you should consider in your presentation:

- Look The Part

You may have heard the saying, 'Image is everything.' This is a fact. I was once invited to be part of a panel of interviewers by a business owner. During the interview process, a particular young female candidate spoke with a lot of conviction but her physical appearance

159

sent the message of a disorganized person as she looked unkempt. Her appearance was her undoing. She did not look the part. She was not given the job.

Your image from head to toe makes a big difference. How you appear affects the way people perceive you. Through your choice of clothes, grooming and general appearance, you make a statement about what kind of person you are. The way you look on the outside is a representation of how you see yourself on the inside. And people judge you mostly by the way you look on the outside. You have to make effort to look the part. Dress the way a highly successful and sought after problem solver would dress. If you need to, read about dressing to learn what works best. Your hair should be well kept, your nails manicured. Walk briskly. Look enthusiastic. You have to cultivate the image of a professional who is likeable and can be trusted to provide the needed solution.

- Get and Keep Their Attention

There are two ways to sum up the interests of employers/customers: they desire gains and abhor losses. These are the two things that can grab and keep their attention. During your presentation, if you can show them how their profits will improve to a new level, they will hire you. If you can show them the financial loss you would save them, they will also hire you. Just make sure that what you show is measurable. For instance, you can call their attention to how much money they will make and save if your service reduces their project delivery time by 30 percent. Or you can let them know how your service can increase product sales by 20 percent. Of course, that money goes to their bottom line. If you can capture this in your presentation an employer/customer will be interested in getting your service.

160

You can sum up your sales success in this simple formula: C + P = EP. **C** stands for **Content**, that is, the relevant skill or expertise. **P** stands for **Presentation**. **EP** stands for **Employer's Perception**. If the employer's/customer's perception of you is positive, you will most likely get the job.

INCREASE YOUR PRODUCTIVITY

Most employees do just enough to get paid. They are more interested in their benefits than their productivity; more concerned with their (lunch) breaks than their customers. But in today's marketplace, there is no room for anyone who is not prepared to work hard to solve problems. There is no place for anyone who will not give their best to contribute value. You have to increase your productivity. If you don't, employers/customer will eventually tell you *sorry, no vacancy*. Here are a few things you can do to increase your productivity:

- Spend Your Work Hours Actually Working

Giving in to distractions at work can greatly undermine your productivity. It might be fun spending work time chatting with colleagues, reading the newspaper, making personal phone calls or surfing the internet, but these activities add little or no value to your employers/customers.

Some people delude themselves into thinking they are actually working when they engage in low value and no value activities that do not solve any meaningful problem. When you work, work! Concentrate on high value tasks that solve problems for employer/customers. Engage yourself with the problems you have been hired to solve. Don't get sidetracked by activities that provide no value. Focus on result-producing activities.

- Give More

The only certain means to getting your desired reward is to render more and better service than is expected of you, no matter what your task may be. Remember the story of the two brothers and the fish farm. The father paid the younger brother more because he always did more than he was told to do. Always go the extra mile when you provide solutions to employers/customers. You may have to come in earlier than others to get more work done. You may have to skip lunch to get an important project finished on schedule. You may have to work late because your employer/customer needs you to help with an urgent task or assignment.

It pays to give more as a problem solver. Lee Iacocca, the former chairman of the Chrysler Corporation, said, "The kind of people I look for to fill top management spots are the eager beavers, the mavericks. These are the guys who try to do more than they are expected to do." All employers look for such people to fill top positions in their organization. Giving more is the secret to getting promoted faster and being paid more. When you give more you will eventually get more rewards. This is in consonance with the law of sowing and reaping. If you sow little, you reap little. But if you sow more, you reap more.

- Offer Better Solutions

You need to strive for excellence (the outstanding and superior) when you provide solutions. Aim to always go above and beyond expectations. Get better and offer better solutions. You have to push yourself to rise above every tendency for mediocrity and demonstrate excellence. You have to become a game changer in the marketplace and offer more innovative solutions.

Set standards of excellent performance for yourself. Strive continually to be better at your job. Excellence is a commitment to continually providing better solutions. Whenever your work is compared with that of others let it stand out as 'better.' Every job speaks of the one who did it. So any time you are solving problems, make consistent effort to autograph your work with excellence.

- Become Faster

Employers/customers want their problems solved quickly and are willing to pay more for fast solutions. Fast food restaurants attract lots of customers because they solve people's need for food, fast. People pay more for express laundry service because they get their clothes cleaned and delivered faster. People want faster internet connections, want their cars washed faster, and want to get in and out of the banking hall faster. If you can solve a problem faster you will develop a reputation as the person that can be depended on to get the job done when it matters most. This can get you paid more and promoted faster in the workplace.

STAY DISCIPLINED

Making a mind shift, developing yourself and taking necessary action to produce desirable results take effort. It requires self-discipline —the ability to compel yourself to do what you should do when you should do it, whether you feel like it or not. Self-discipline is what ensures you follow through and stay on until you get results.

Jim Rohn submits: "Discipline is the bridge between goals and accomplishments." Mark Sanborn expounds, "Discipline is the connective tissue between an idea and result. It's the muscle that takes what you know and converts it to what you enjoy." For you to get from the point of taking the first step toward your goal to the point where you get your desired reward you need to stay disciplined. Succeeding isn't easy. If it were, everyone would be successful. But just because something is hard doesn't mean it is unattainable. If you can discipline yourself to stay put and get the knowledge, skill and competence that will enable you become a problem solver, and apply them to provide value, you will earn the rewards meant for you as a solution provider.

WHO YOU ARE DETERMINES YOUR REWARD

Once upon a time two young men, Seenone and Seefar, were told by their father, Seeall, to travel to a city called Richland where there was wealth awaiting them. With excitement, Seenone took off as fast as he could so he could get there first and grab much of the wealth before his brother arrived. After a long journey, Seenone came to the city. He saw people indiscriminately dumping refuse everywhere and living in chaos. He looked around but saw no form of wealth. He was upset that his father had made him come to Richland for nothing, and he thought, "What filth! I need to get out of this place." Seenone went back home and complained to his father that there was no wealth in Richland, only filth and chaos.

Meanwhile Seefar got to the same city after his brother had left and thought, "What filth! I think I can provide a solution. I'll start a refuse collection business and clean up this mess." He became wealthy by collecting and properly disposing of the refuse in the city. He did so well cleaning and organizing the city that the people decided to make him the chairman of the city council. Seefar invited his father and brother to come celebrate with him on his appointment as chairman.

When Seenone and their father got to Richland Seenone was amazed at the city's transformation. And even more astonishing was the wealth his brother had accumulated and the honour he had been accorded in Richland. As Seenone wondered how this had come about, their father turned to him and said, "Who you are determines your reward."

In his book, *Developing the Leader Within You*, John Maxwell says: "My observation is that people don't like problems, weary of them quickly, and will do almost anything to get away from them. This climate makes others place the reins of leadership into your hands —if you are willing and are able to either tackle their problems or train them to solve them. Your problem-solving skills will always be needed, because people always have problems."

You can become a problem solver if you choose to be one. You have what it takes. All you need to do is make a shift in your mindset and choose to become a solution provider to any of the many problems employers/customers have. Of course, this will earn you rewards. So the question now is who do you choose to be, a problem solver or part of the problem? Beginning from today, take action towards establishing yourself as a problem solver and there will always be vacancy just for you.

THIS IS COMMON SENSE

1.   You are the answer to the problems of employers/customers.

2. You have to hold yourself accountable to produce results.

3. You need to do what it takes to become the answer to employers' or customers' problems.

4. You must show yourself as the answer to your employer's or customer's problems.

5. You must continually increase your productivity by working hard to provide more, better and faster solutions.

6. When you position yourself as the answer to problems, employers and customers will always have a vacancy for you. This means you get to earn the rewards you desire.

ACTION EXERCISES

1. Write down these words and repeat them to yourself: 'I'm a provider of solutions.'

2. Write down the steps you will take to actualize this affirmation.

3. Write down the steps you will take to reinforce this perception in the mind of your employer/customer.

CONCLUSION

COMMIT TO STANDING AND FINISHING

A man who takes advice is still a man acting on his own free will.

- Nigerian proverb

The advice that best captures what you have to do to reap the benefits of this book can be found in these words from Apostle Paul in the Bible: "…And having done all, to stand." What we have provided for you is liberating information. However, for it to work you need to commit to applying it. You have to learn the principles in this book, act on them, hold on and not let go. Do not allow yourself to return to your former ways of thinking and acting.

There are numerous books about success and how to achieve it. Authors, speakers and coaches on the subject abound, yet there is very little that people can show by way of lasting impact. Individuals and corporations pay lots of money yearly to train people on personal effectiveness, success, leadership, entrepreneurship and getting ahead in life. Often times people get excited and fired up during these seminars, conferences and training sessions. Some seminar or conference facilitators even insist that participants write down action plans that they intend to follow once they get back to their work desks or homes. But by the end of six months more than three quarters revert to old behaviours and only intermittently remember to practice one or two aspects of what they have been taught. They do not press on to get their reward.

The difference between getting ahead, stagnating or receding is to actually stand. Brian Tracy calls it "courageous patience —the ability to hang in there and continue working and fighting after you have gone all in and before you have yet seen any results or rewards." Standing depicts ability and readiness to practice what you have read or been taught in a dogged manner. A resolve to put to use the principles expounded in this book. A willingness and belief in the need to stand out so badly that you are willing to keep on practicing. You actively seek out ways and opportunities to inculcate the ideas contained in this book and track your progress.

The bottom line is this: having spent your money on this book, you need to reap the benefits by practicing the principles and becoming that highly sought after problem solver. You need to be firmly resolved to constantly practise the principles you have learned in this book. You will need this kind of resolve to become a highly sought after problem solver.

THE LAW OF TWOS

For any individual to succeed there are certain attributes and concepts that must be internalized. These attributes and concepts usually come in twos, with one complementing the other. The law of twos says that every individual by nature has one of these and must adopt and grow the other for them to succeed.

To help you reach your goal, it is important to practice the Law of Twos to ensure you stand out in a positive way and for the right reasons. As human beings, we are endowed with one of these two attributes, and sometimes in great abundance. But we are required to work hard on the other one lest we make a mess of the ability given to us to solve problems and profit. Here are some of the laws:

1. Confidence Without Humility Leads to Arrogance and Pride

Have you ever come across the term intellectual arrogance? There have been interview sessions where certain candidates leave the room and everyone on the interview panel comes to the same conclusion: this candidate is qualified and fits the role but is intellectually arrogant and will be a disruptive force within the team. Therefore, we cannot hire him. Such candidates rarely get to know the true reason they were not hired.

Confidence is good and superior knowledge even better; however, if this is not tempered with humility, you tend to come across as arrogant or proud and most people do not get along with the proud. It is extremely important to be self-confident but ensure that it goes with humility. Nothing is as endearing as a very knowledgeable person who is humble.

2. Power Without Control Leads to Disaster

When you are put in a position of authority and power, it is important that you have not only self-control but also external control measures to ensure that you do not abuse the power and cause mayhem. Organizations and certain systems understand this principle and therefore put checks in place. In a democracy, the principle of checks and balances ensures that no single organ of government is all-powerful and that the arms of government can put each other in check. In the words of Lord Acton, "Power tends to corrupt and absolute power corrupts absolutely. Great men are almost always bad men, even when they exercise influence and not authority; still more when you super add the tendency of the certainty of corruption by authority."

No one individual, no matter how reasonable, should be vested with absolute power even in a business organization. This is why the principle of corporate governance (internal to organizations) exists. And for external checks, each corporate body is subject to the control of regulatory bodies. The Managing Director is in charge of the company but is ultimately responsible to the Board of Directors, which has a Chairman. The Board of Directors is in turn responsible to regulatory bodies. This principle is extremely important for someone who wants to be successful. If you wish to start out as an entrepreneur, I urge you to incorporate this principle into the very fabric of your endeavour as it will help you build a lasting business.

3. Hard work Without Smartness Leads to Frustration

The hardest worker is not usually the most well recognised or highly paid. In fact, most hard workers do not get well paid except they inject some level of smartness. A bricklayer works much harder than an architect who sits in the comfort of his office working on AutoCAD to design his edifice. Also, an Architect who does not know how to use any of the design applications/software will spend twice the time or more working on the same building design as an architect using a design application. However, the pay will not necessarily be higher for the architect who works 'manually'. Instead, the architect who uses design software is more likely to be paid more because by working smarter he will save his employer/customer time and money in the long run. Employers/customers expect you to work hard but it pays to work smart as well.

4. Speed Without Direction Leads to 'Error at the T-Junction' and Lots of Reworks

Prof. F.E Ogbimi of the Technology Policy Development Unit (TPDU) at the Obafemi Awolowo University, Ile Ife, propounded the principle of 'Error at the T-Junction', and it is apt in understanding speed without direction leading to reworks. Imagine that two runners start a race at a particular point, and 2km from the start point they get to a T-Junction. A decision has to be made as to whether to go left or right. If the finish line is at the end of the right turn about 5km away, and the left turn leads to a dead end 5km later, then even if the faster runner takes the left turn he would have made an error at the T-Junction. He would then have to run a total of 17km to get to the finish line as he would have gone an additional 10km just travelling in the wrong direction and back to the decision making point (the T-Junction). The runner who makes the right turn the first time is likely to win because he had only 7km to run.

Direction is very important. Even if you have the gift of speed, seek direction before the journey begins or you might cost yourself, employers/customers, sponsors and investors lots of money and time, and nobody likes this.

5. A Dream Without Commensurate Action is a Mere Illusion

Many dreamers are lazy about pursuing their dreams. They usually are good at portraying the picture of Eldorado but somehow seem unable to get there. The ability to dream big is a great gift, but you need to add to that the grit and sweat to ensure you get to your dreamland. Otherwise it remains a daydream and sometimes may even lead to

171

nightmares. Add to your ability to dream the action required to make those dreams happen.

6. Passion Without Mission Leads to Nuisance

People who possess passion but lack the mission to appropriately channel their energy end up being disruptive to others. Passion is a gift that many lack. Therefore, if you are blessed with the gift of passion, find out what is important to you and go after it. Do some research on relevant issues around you; you may find direction and a mission to bring your passion to bear upon. If you do not have a mission that adds value to humanity, you may end up being a nuisance to people.

7. Mission Without Vision Leads Nowhere

Have you met people who say they want to do grand things but have no vision for it because they are not convinced? They tout the words of others and therefore are on a journey with no conviction. When times become tough and the terrain gets rough, they are usually the first to turn back because they never had a vision in the first place. Mission without a vision backing it usually gets aborted and leads nowhere.

In conclusion, everyone is blessed naturally with one of these two pronged forks, but we are expected to work on the other diligently in order to be productive and effective. Find out which one comes naturally to you and which one you need to work on. It may be the key to that door you have been knocking on for a while. It may be the key to you becoming the problem solver that your country needs. It may be the key to your hearing the words 'You are urgently needed.'

Made in the USA
San Bernardino, CA
28 November 2016